The Sirtfood Diet 3.0:

The Complete Guide To Cooking On The Sirt Food Diet Using The Secret Of The Famous Skinny Gene! Over 50 Easy, Healthy And Delicious Recipes. |Discover The Celebrities Secrets to Weight-Loss |

| June 2021Edition|

© Copyright 2021 by Brenda Sanchez

Table Of Contents

Introduction 1
Chapter 1: What Is Sirt Diet 4
    Is Sirtfood Diet Good for You? 4
    Is It Effective? 5
    Sirtfood Diet Essentials 7
    Does Sirtfood Diet Have Any Side Effects? 8
Chapter 2: Why Everyone Talking About It 9
    Security and Side Effects 9
    Why it works 10
    Sirtuins Activate Your Body's Wellness Genes 11
    What nourishments initiate sirtuins? 13
Chapter 3: The Sirt Diet Plan 14
    How the Sirtfood diet actually work? 14
    Is there any diet plan that exists for the Sirtfood diet? 14
    What happens after finishing the Sirtfood diet? 14
    How to do the Sirtfood plan? 15
    How does the diet work? 15
The possible cost of Sirtfood diets: 16
Detail of phase one: 17
    Detail of Phase Two: 17
After diet effects: 17
Sirtfood diet plan does exist: 18
    *First week: 18
    *Second week: 18
Chapter 4: The Sciences Behind Sirt Diet 19
Is There A Quick Fix? 20
As a matter of first importance, what the hell is a sirtfood? 21
Chapter 5: Activation of Sirtuins 23
    A Passion for Exercise? 24
Enter Sirtfoods 24
    Dealing with the Fat 25
    Lean Genes 25
    Fat Busting 26
    Wat or Bat 26
Chapter 6: Calorie Restriction and Lifespan 28
    The mysteries of thinness 28
    Slimming is linked to genetics 28
    Target these genes to avoid obesity 29
    The super regulators of metabolism 29
    A point in common among the healthiest diets in the world 30
Chapter 7: Foods to Activate Sirtuins 32
    Beyond antioxidants 32
Chapter 8: Top 20 SIRT Foods 34
Chapter 9: The Potential Health and Weight Loss Benefits 38
Chapter 10: Empowering Yourself with Sirt Foods Building a Diet That Works 41
Chapter 11: How to Follow the Sirt Diet 45

- Phase One and Phase Two? 45
- The First Step 45
- The second phase 45
- What are sirtuins? 46
- The science of sirt food 47

Chapter 12: Succeeding with Phase One 49

Chapter 13: Research Your Goal in Phase Two 53

Chapter 14: How to Continue Managing Your Weight Returning to Three Meals . 55
- Sirtfood Bites 55
- "Sirtifying" Your Meals 56
- Cooking for More 57

Q&A 57
- Is Sirtfood healthy for children? 57
- Can I Exercise During Stage One? 58
- Can You Eat Meat and Dairy on The Sirtfood Diet? 59
- Can I Drink Red Wine during Stage One? 59

Chapter 15: Breakfast Recipes Sirtfood 60
- Mushroom Scramble Eggs 60
- Blue Hawaii Smoothie 61
- Turkey Breakfast Sausages 62
- Banana Pecan Muffins 63
- Banana and Blueberry Muffins - SRC 64
- Morning Meal Sausage Gravy 65
- Easy Egg-White Muffins 66
- Sweet Potato Hash 67
- Asparagus, Mushroom Artichoke Strata 68
- Egg White Veggie Wontons W/Fontina Topped W/ Crispy Prosciutto 69

Chapter 16: Power Juice and Cocktail Recipes 70
- Lemonade Redneck 70
- Coffee Latte Milkshake 71
- Berry and Beet Smoothie 72
- Green Pineapple Smoothie 73
- Blue Hawaii 74
- Daiquiri 75
- Spinach Smoothie 76
- Kale Smoothie 77
- Avocado Smoothie 78
- Lettuce Smoothie 79

Chapter 17: Main Meal Recipes 80
- Baked Potatoes with Spicy Chickpea Stew Fillet Diablo 80
- Artichoke-Stuffed Red Snapper 81
- Sesame Chicken Salad 82
- Sirt Food Miso-Marinated Cod with Stir-Fried Greens 83
- Raspberry and Blackcurrant Jelly-Sirtfood Recipes 84
- Strawberry Buckwheat Tabouleh 85
- Buckwheat and Nut Loaf 86
- Moong Dahl 87
- Polenta Bake 88
- Cajun Steak and Veg Rice Jar Recipe 89

Chapter Eighteen: Stir Fry Recipes 90
- Chicken and Green Beans 90

Moo Goo Gai Pan (Mushrooms with Chicken) 91
Garlic Chicken 92
Cashew Chicken 93
Creamy Curry Chicken with Vegetables 94
Simple Beef Stir-fry 95
Easy Shiitake Stir-fry 96
Okra Stir-fry 97
Simple Stir-Fried Bok Choy 98
Lettuce Stir-fry 99

Chapter 19: Sweets 100
Dark Chocolate Mousse (Vegan) 100
Loaded Chocolate Fudge 101
Chocolate Maple Walnuts 102
Matcha and Chocolate Dipped Strawberries 103
Oatmeal Raisin Cookies 104
Coconut Cream Tart 105
Apple Pie 106
Blueberry Cream Pie 107
Mocha Chocolate Mousse 108
Mediterranean Scones 109

Chapter 20: Exercises to Do 110

Chapter 21: Phase One Meal Plan 114
Phase 1: 7 pounds in 7 days 114
Phase 1 plan: 114
Tips to get started 115
Phase Two Meal Plan 117

Conclusion 120

© **Copyright 2021 by Brenda Sanchez**

All rights reserved. No part of this guide may be reproduced in any form without permission in writing from the publisher except in the case of brief quotations embodied in critical articles or reviews.

Legal & Disclaimer

The information contained in this book and its contents is not designed to replace or take the place of any form of medical or professional advice; and is not meant to replace the need for independent medical, financial, legal or other professional advice or services, as may be required. The content and information in this book have been provided for educational and entertainment purposes only.

The content and information contained in this book has been compiled from sources deemed reliable, and it is accurate to the best of the Author's knowledge, information and belief. However, the Author cannot guarantee its accuracy and validity and cannot be held liable for any errors and/or omissions. Further, changes are periodically made to this book as and when needed. Where appropriate and/or necessary, you must consult a professional (including but not limited to your doctor, attorney, financial advisor or such other professional advisor) before using any of the suggested remedies, techniques, or information in this book.

Upon using the contents and information contained in this book, you agree to hold harmless the Author from and against any damages, costs, and expenses, including any legal fees potentially resulting from the application of any of the information provided by this book. This disclaimer applies to any loss, damages or injury caused by the use and application, whether directly or indirectly, of any advice or information presented, whether for breach of contract, tort, negligence, personal injury, criminal intent, or under any other cause of action.

You agree to accept all risks of using the information presented inside this book.

You agree that by continuing to read this book, where appropriate and/or necessary, you shall consult a professional (including but not limited to your doctor, attorney, or financial advisor or such other advisor as needed) before using any of the suggested remedies, techniques, or information in this book.

Introduction

This Diet relies on research sirtuins (SIRTs), a set of seven proteins utilized from the human anatomy that's been proven to modulate various purposes, including inflammation, metabolism, and life span.

Certain Natural plant chemicals could possibly find a way to grow the degree of those proteins inside the human anatomy, and foods containing them are known "sirtfoods."

The Diet blends sirtfoods and calorie limitation, both of which may possibly cause the human body to generate high degrees of sirtuins.
The Sirtfood Diet publication comprises meal plans and recipes to follow along; however, there are lots of additional Sirtfood Diet recipe collections out there.

The Diet's founders claim that after a Sirtfood Diet can cause accelerated body weight loss while maintaining muscles and protecting you in chronic illness.
Once You've finished the dietary plan, you're invited to keep on adding sirtfoods and also the diet signature green juice to your normal diet.

Thus Much, there aren't any persuasive signs that the Sirtfood Diet features a more favorable impact on weight loss than every other calorie-restricted diet regime.

Along with Although a number of those foods have healthy properties, there have yet to be any long-term human studies to ascertain if eating a diet full of sirtfoods has some concrete health benefits.

Nonetheless, the Sirtfood Diet publication reports the outcomes of a pilot study conducted with both the writers and between 3 9 participants in their exercise center.

Nevertheless, the consequences of the study appear never to have already been released somewhere else.

To get 1 week, the participants followed the diet and worked out each day. At the close of the week, the participants lost an average of 5 pounds (3.2 kg) and claimed even gained muscle tissue.

Yet These outcomes are hardly surprising. Restricting your own calorie intake to 1000 calories and exercising at the exact same period will almost always trigger weight loss.

No matter This type of fast fat reduction is neither true nor long-term, which analysis failed to accompany participants following the initial week to determine whether they attained some of the weight, and this is an average of the situation.

When Your own body is energy-deprived, it melts away its catastrophe energy stores, or glycogen, along with burning off muscle and fat.

Each Molecule of glycogen necessitates 3--4 atoms of water to bestow. Whenever your body melts away glycogen, then it eliminates the water too. It's referred to as "water".

The very first week of extreme calorie limit, just about one-fifth of those fat loss arises from fat, whereas one other two-thirds stems out of water, glycogen, and muscle.

When your calories grow, the own body accomplishes its own glycogen stores, and also, the weight comes back again.

Regrettably, such a calorie restriction may also cause the human body to reduce its metabolism, which makes it need fewer calories every day for energy compared earlier.

Additionally, it Is very likely that diet might help you drop a couple of pounds at the start, although it is going to probably return once the diet has ended.

As Much as preventing illness, three weeks might be long enough to own some measurable long-term effects.

The flip side, adding sirtfoods to a routine diet within the long-term, might just be a fantastic idea. However, in this circumstance, you may too, bypass the diet and begin doing this today.

Chapter 1: What Is Sirt Diet

Sirtfood Diet was developed in the United Kingdom by two nutritionists who were working at a private gym. They marketed the diet as a "revolutionary new diet" and health strategy that works by switching on the "skinny gene" in the human body system.

The Sirtfood diet is the latest way to burn extreme body fat and lose weight dramatically without having to experience malnutrition or starve oneself.

Activating the skinny gene is achieved through exercising and fasting. There are some categories of foods that have chemicals known as polyphenols that when consumed, they put little stress on the body cells. Thus, producing genes that imitate the consequences of both fasting and exercise. Certain foods have high polyphenols present in them such as dark chocolate (cocoa), coffee, red wine, kale and so on. When these kinds of foods are taken, they tend to release Sirtuins reactions that influence aging, mood and metabolism. Any diet high in Sirtfoods triggers weight loss without necessarily having to expend muscles, while at the same time maintaining a healthy lifestyle and health.

This particular diet focuses on calorie restriction which is in phases. This calorie restriction is believed to increase the production of Sirtuins in the body.

Is Sirtfood Diet Good for You?

Every food on the diet plan is very healthy for you. You stand to get the right amount of nutrients, vitamins, minerals and which will likely become high when following this diet. This diet is very restrictive on some kinds of foods and calories and this may make it a bit difficult for some people to follow and get accustomed to.

Is It Effective?

The developers of the diet are so positive about the wonders this diet performs in weight loss, in burning fat, in activating the body's skinny gene and in the inhibition of health-related conditions. The only concern is there's little proof to back these.

Conversely, there is no convincing evidence to ascertain the diet's beneficial effects on weight loss than any other type of food or diet restricted by calories. Nonetheless, many of the foods in this diet are rich in nutrients, minerals, and vitamins but there are no human studies to determine whether eating a diet high in Sirtfoods has any reasonable health benefits.

Contrarily to this, the Sirtfood Diet states the results derived from a pilot study the authors conducted which involved 39 participants from their gym. The result of this study was not published in any other source.

For the first week, the participants were put on a strict daily diet and exercise. By the end of the first week, the participants have recorded an average of 7 pounds weight loss. Achieving this result is not surprising at all, the reason being that restricting your calorie consumption to 1,000 calories coupled with exercise will result in weight loss.

Nonetheless, this kind of weight loss is not genuine and long-lasting. There was no evidence to determine if there was any follow up to know whether the participants gained back the weight, which is most likely to be the case. The key to this kind of diet is continuity. You have to keep following this diet until you have achieved your desired weight goal and then keep maintaining it over and over again. In the absence of this, the moment you make a sudden swerve from this diet, you are very much likely to gain those weight back.

When the body experiences energy deprivation, it utilizes either glycogen or its stored emergency energy and this is in addition to muscle loss and fat burning.

In a nutshell, Sirtfood Diet is likely to help you lose weight virtually because it's low in calories. But be prepared to gain the weight back once the diet is over. This is because the diet is very short to have a long-term effect on your body.

Sirtfood Diet Essentials

- *The diet consists of twenty highly rated foods, which you can combine with your everyday meal.*
- **Buckwheat**: *This is available in the form of noodles and fruit seed. It's in every way different from wheat. So, when getting yours, it should be 100 percent buckwheat.*
- **Celery:** *Very nutritious especially the hearts and the leaves. Always blend hem together.*
- **Extra virgin olive oil**: *This is a very top ingredient in SIRTFOOD DIET. It has a peppery taste and it's highly sirtifying.*
- **Bird's eye chili**: *Also known as Thai chili. They are hotter than regular chilis and have more nutrients.*
- **Capers:** *Good for salad.*
- **Green tea or matcha:** *Very soothing when combined with a slice of lemon.*
- **Cocoa:** *Helps in the control of blood sugar, cholesterol and blood pressure.*
- **Kale:** *It's a very high SIRTUINS activator. Rich in quercetin and kaempferol.*
- **Parsley:** *Sprinkle it on your meals, juice or smoothie. It's far more than just a mere garnish.*
- **Lovage**
- **Red onion**
- **Strawberries**
- **Chicory**
- **Turmeric**
- **Soy**
- **Red wine**
- **Walnuts**
- **Soy**
- **Medjool dates**
- **Rocket**

Does Sirtfood Diet Have Any Side Effects?

First and foremost, the diet has no room for substitutions. Sirtfood Diet is very limiting and restrictive. It counts calories and focuses on a certain food category.

Even though the SIRTFOOD recommended meals may look yummy and tasty, the diet is likely to be deficient in major nutrients like iron, zinc and calcium. They are not the kind of meal you will most likely find on the "list of healthy food" says an anonymous nutritionist. Eating a little bar of chocolate and having a glass of red wine is no bad thing and won't affect the body in any way. However, it shouldn't be an everyday thing. Eating varieties of fruits and vegetables is better and not just the ones recommended on the list.

Also, the weight loss can only be maintained only if the calorie restriction is also maintained otherwise, the weight comes right back. It takes time to burn fat and lose weight, there's no doubt about this. It's evident that this kind of weight loss is most likely to be that of fluid and not fat. The moment people go back to their former lifestyle and eating habit, the weight will be back in a matter of time, except if this is long term diet.

In essence, if you are not the type that skips food regulary, especially during the day, you are very much likely to experience some difficulties such as dizziness, headaches, nausea, inability to concentrate

Chapter 2: Why Everyone Talking About It

Propelled initially in 2016, the Sirtfood diet stays a hotly debated issue and includes supporters receiving an eating routine rich in 'sirtfoods'. As per the eating regimen's organizers, these exceptional nourishments work by enacting explicit proteins in the body called sirtuins. Sirtuins are accepted to shield cells in the body from kicking the bucket when they are under pressure and are thought to manage irritation, digestion and the maturing procedure. It's the idea that sirtuins impact the body's capacity to consume fat and lift digestion, bringing about seven-pound weight reduction seven days while looking after muscle. In any case, a few specialists accept this is probably not going to be an exclusively fat misfortune, however, it will rather reflect changes in glycogen stores from skeletal muscle and the liver.

Security and Side Effects

Despite the fact that the main period of the Sirtfood Diet is low in calories and healthfully deficient, there are no genuine security worries for the normal, solid grown-up thinking about the eating regimen's brief span.

However, for somebody with diabetes, calorie limitation and drinking generally squeeze for the initial scarcely any days of the eating regimen may cause risky changes in glucose levels.

All things considered, even a solid individual may encounter some reactions — essentially hunger.

Eating just 1,000–1,500 calories for each day will leave pretty much anybody feeling hungry, particularly if quite a bit of what you're expending is juice, which is low in fiber, a supplement that helps keep you feeling full.

During stage one, you may encounter opposite reactions, for example, weakness, dazedness and crabbiness because of the calorie limitation.

For the in any case sound grown-up, genuine wellbeing outcomes are improbable if the eating regimen is followed for just three weeks.

Sirtfoods are generally plant-based and high in cell reinforcements that help stunt your body into consuming fat at a higher rate. It's called Sirt on the grounds that it incorporates eating nourishments that are high in sirtuin activators, characterized as seven proteins found in the body that control digestion, aggravation, and the life span of cells. Created by two British Nutritionists, Aidan Goggins and Glen Matten, the nourishments should actuate your body's "thin quality" to consume fat quicker. They wrote the "official" direct: The Official Sirtfood Diet.

Why it works

Sirt nourishments help signal the body that it should fire up your digestion and increment bulk while you consume fat. Otherwise called superfoods, the main 20 sirtfoods incorporate the rundown underneath. Note that everybody gets amped up for the wine and chocolate however your body is entirely eating more fiber, more cancer prevention agents, and supplement thick nourishments.

Sirtuins Activate Your Body's Wellness Genes

People groups have consistently been interested in the 'Wellspring of Youth' and how we can live more and more advantageous lives. All things considered, established researchers have an equivalent interest with a group of qualities called sirtuins. All of us houses sirtuins—frequently alluded to as our thin qualities—and they are really entrancing, holding the ability to decide things like our capacity to consume fat and remain thin, our vulnerability to ailment, and even to what extent, we can live.

So, what makes sirtuins so ground-breaking?

Sirtuins are unique in light of their capacity to change our phones to a sort of endurance mode— setting off an incredible reusing process that gets out cell waste and consumes fat. The advantages of this are quite marvelous: Fat melts away and we become fitter, less fatty, and more beneficial.

So how would we exploit sirtuins?

This brings up the issue: What would we be able to do to actuate sirtuins and receive these stunning rewards? It is notable that both fasting and exercise initiate sirtuins. In any case, oh, both interest a steadfast duty to either food limitation or requesting exercise systems. Reducing calories leaves us feeling exhausted, hungry, and strongly cantankerous, and in the more drawn out term can prompt muscle misfortune and stale digestion. With respect to work out, the sum should have been powerful for weight reduction requires a LOT of exertion.

Both can be difficult to achieve.

In 2013, the consequences of one of the loftiest dietary investigations at any point did were distributed. The reason for the investigation, called PREDIMED, was flawlessly basic: It examined the distinction between a Mediterranean-style diet enhanced with either extra-virgin olive oil or nuts and an increasingly regular present-day diet. Results demonstrated that following five years, coronary illness and diabetes were cut by an unbelievable 30 percent, alongside significant decreases in the danger of weight in the Mediterranean eating routine gathering.

This wasn't unexpected, however when the examination was researched in more noteworthy detail it was found there was no distinction in calorie, fat, or starch admission between the two gatherings. How would you clarify that?

Not every (sound) food are made equivalent.

Research currently shows that plants contain common mixes called polyphenols that have colossal advantages for our wellbeing. What's more, when scientists dissecting PREDIMED examined polyphenol utilization among the members, the outcomes were faltering. Over simply the five-year time frame, the individuals who expended the most elevated levels of polyphenols had 37 percent less passing contrasted with the individuals who ate the least.

Be that as it may, not all polyphenols are equivalent. Information out of Harvard University from more than 124,000 people demonstrated that solitary certain polyphenols were useful for weight control. Also, an investigation of right around 3,000 twins found that a higher admission of just certain polyphenols was connected with less muscle to fat ratio and a more advantageous dispersion of fat in the body. Polyphenols are without a doubt a shelter for remaining thin and solid, yet in the event that not all polyphenols are equivalent, at that point which are the best? Might it be able to be those that exploration has demonstrated have the capacity to turn on our sirtuin qualities? Exactly the same ones enacted by fasting and exercise?

The pharmaceutical business has rushed to abuse these sirtuin-actuating supplements, contributing several millions to change over them into panacea drugs. For instance, the well-known diabetes medicate metformin originates from a plant and actuates our sirtuin qualities. In any case, up to this point they have been to a great extent ignored by the universe of sustenance, to the weakness of our wellbeing and our waistlines.

What nourishments initiate sirtuins?

With our advantage provoked we put all the nourishments with the most elevated levels of sirtuin-enacting polyphenols together into a unique eating regimen. This incorporates extra-virgin olive oil and pecans, the particular considerations in PREDIMED, just as arugula, red onions, strawberries, red wine, dim chocolate, green tea, and espresso among numerous others. At the point when we pilot tried it, the outcomes were shocking. Members shed pounds, while either keeping up or in any event, expanding their bulk. The best part is that individuals revealed feeling incredible—overflowing with vitality, dozing better, and with eminent upgrades in their skin.

Thus, the Sirtfood Diet was conceived, a progressive better approach to initiate sirtuins by eating heavenly nourishments. An eating routine that doesn't include calorie excluding, removing carbs, or eating low fat. An eating routine of incorporation in which you receive the rewards from eating the nourishments your adoration. The Sirtfood Diet is rocking the boat of good dieting counsel and what it truly intends to look and feel extraordinary. And all from eating our preferred nourishments!

Chapter 3: The Sirt Diet Plan

The nutritionists had developed the Sirtfood Diet. They were so interested in Sirtfoods' ability; they developed a diet focused on optimizing the consumption of Sirtfood and limiting mild calories. They then checked this diet on exclusive London workout participants and were shocked by their results. In the first seven days, gym participants dropped a total of 7lbs, despite not growing their workout rates. The participants not only shed a large amount of weight but also added strength (usually the reverse occurs while dieting) and registered major changes in physical health and well-being.

How the Sirtfood diet actually work?

The food is split down into two stages. Phase 1: the 'hyper success phase' of 7 days, incorporating a Sirtfood-rich diet with mild calorie restriction, and Phase 2: the 'maintenance phase' of 14 days, where you maintain the weight loss without reducing calories.

Is there any diet plan that exists for the Sirtfood diet?

Yeah, the is a handy map that shows you what you should consume every day, and when. It contains all the recipes that you'll require for the first three weeks. There's a meat/fish alternative for any day and a vegetarian/vegan choice. Nearly all of the meals are gluten-free, and dairy-free choices are accessible every day, ensuring that this is a lifestyle that should operate for most people.

What happens after finishing the Sirtfood diet?

The Sirtfood Diet is not meant as a one-off 'diet' but rather as a way of life. You are encouraged to continue eating a diet rich in Sirtfoods once you've completed the first three weeks and continue drinking your daily green juice.

How to do the Sirtfood plan?

The eating schedule describes the twenty foods that turn on the so-called 'skinny genes' to increase metabolism and energy rates. This simply stipulates you can lose 7lbs in 7 days.

The diet strategy will change the way you eat well. This seems like a name that is not user friendly, but it's something that you are likely to learn for a lot. Since the 'Sirt' is slang for the sirtuin genes in Sirtfoods, a community of genes called the 'skinny genes' that function, literally, like magic.

Eating certain items, the plan's developers claim, flips certain genes on, and mimics the results of calorie restriction, fasting, and exercise. It triggers a cycle of regeneration in the body, filtering out the cellular waste and garbage that accumulates over time and induces ill health and strength loss.

How does the diet work?

Sirtfoods function by triggering the body's so-called "skinny gene" receptors, the same genes that are triggered while we are exercising or fast. This makes the body lose fat in a manner that mimics the limit on calories, even without the lack of nutrients or other deficiencies.

The group of people studying the diet, including improved muscle mass and signs of feeling complete and happy with food consumption, showed an overall loss of 7 pounds of weight in 7 days.

Sirtfoods function as master regulators of our metabolism as a whole, most importantly having effects on fat burning while at the same time rising muscle and enhancing cellular health. Some of the items falling within the Sirfood grouping are also often aligned with the world's healthiest diets-such as the traditional Mediterranean diet. The program has two stages, with the first being the most intensive aspect of '7ibs-in-7-days' with the second going further at the side of things in terms of maintenance. The special foods trigger sirtuins (SIRTs), a group of 7 proteins found in the body which regulate the cycle of metabolism, inflammation, and aging. These specific proteins are believed to defend cells from dying due to stress. Researchers also conclude that sirtuins improve the body's capacity to lose fat and raise metabolism. Some plant compounds can increase the body level of those proteins. Foods that contain these compounds are called "sirt foods."

The possible cost of Sirtfood diets:

You just have to prepare and have access to the correct ingredients to adopt your diet properly. You will need to invest in a proper juicer too, which will run you at least $100. You will need to invest in some of The Sirtfood Diet collections, in addition to the free recipes available on the website.

The seasonality of products makes having strawberries and kale a little difficult at some periods of the year. Continuing on while driving, at social gatherings, and feeding a family of small children is always difficult.

The diet itself leaves off multiple food classes and is restrictive. Dairy products are not included on the menu and contain an assortment of important nutrients, including some that most people miss. Furthermore, the polyphenol-rich food matcha also contains lead in the tea leaves, which, particularly when taken regularly, is potentially harmful to your safety. Like 85 percent dark chocolate, it also has a deep and bitter taste, which is also suggested.

The bottom line:

Surely, polyphenol-rich products should be used in a weight-reduction plan, but they are not the foundation for a whole diet. Of course, you don't need everyday wine and dark chocolate, plus so much matcha is potentially harmful.

Detail of phase one:

The first phase continues for seven days, with calorie control and plenty of green juice included. It's supposed to improve your weight reduction and promise to help you drop 7 pounds (3.2 kg) in seven days.

The intake of calories during the first three days of phase one is limited to 1,000 calories. You consume three green drinks, plus one meal, every day. You will select from recipes here every day, many of which include sirtfood as a big part of the meal.

Detail of Phase Two:

Phase two requires two weeks to finish. You will begin to lose weight slowly through this "maintenance" period.
This stage has no clear calorie cap. Instead, you eat three sirt-food meals and one green juice a day. The meals are again chosen from the recipes included in any guideline.

After diet effects:

These two phases may be repeated as often as you wish for further weight loss. Nonetheless, upon finishing those stages, you are motivated to start "sirtifying" your diet by consistently integrating sirt foods into your meals.

There are a number of Sirtfood Diet publications, full of sirtfood rich recipes. You may also use sirt foods as a snack in your diet, or in recipes that you already have. You are also urged to start consuming the green juice every day. Therefore, the Sirtfood Diet is more a shift of attitude than a one-time diet.

Sirtfood diet plan does exist:

First week:

- *Limit regular consumption to 1k Calories.*
- *Drink three green sirtfood juices a day.*
- *Eat a meal rich in sirtfoods per day.*

Second week:

- Increasing your average consumption to 1.5k calories
- Drink two green sirtfood juices in a day
- Eat double meals per day rich in Sirt foods.
- There is not any fixed strategy at all in the long run. It's more about changing your diet to incorporate as many sirt products as you can, which will help you feel safer and more energy productive.

Chapter 4: The Sciences Behind Sirt Diet

Surely the diet will seem to work for certain individuals. In any case, scientific confirmation of any diet's triumphs is an altogether different issue. Obviously, the perfect investigation to think about the viability of a diet on weight loss (or some other result, for example, maturing) would require an adequately enormous example – delegate of the populace we are keen on – and irregular distribution to a treatment or control gathering. Results would then be checked over enough timeframe with severe command over puzzling factors, for example, different practices that may decidedly or adversely influence the results of enthusiasm (smoking, for example, or work out).

This examination would be constrained by techniques, for example, self-revealing and memory, however, would go some approach to finding the viability of this diet. Research of this nature, be that as it may, doesn't exist and we ought to, therefore, be wary when deciphering essential science – all things considered, human cells in a tissue culture dish presumably respond differently to the phones in a living individual.

Further uncertainty is thrown over this diet when we think about a portion of the specific cases. Losses of seven pounds in a single week are ridiculous and are probably not going to reflect changes to the muscle to fat ratio. For the initial three days, dieters spend around 1000 kcal every day – around 40–half of what a great many people require. This will bring about a fast loss of glycogen (a put-away type of starch) from skeletal muscle and the liver.

Yet, for each gram of put away the glycogen we additionally store roughly 2.7 grams of water, and water is overwhelming. So, for all the lost glycogen, we likewise lose going with water – and henceforth weight. Furthermore, diets that are too prohibitive are difficult to follow and bring about increments in hunger invigorating hormones, for example, ghrelin. Weight (glycogen and water) will therefore come back to typical if the desire to eat wins out.

As a rule, the use of the scientific technique for the investigation of sustenance is difficult. It is often unrealistic to do fake treatment-controlled preliminaries with any level of natural legitimacy, and the wellbeing results that we are often keen on happen over numerous years, making research configuration testing. Besides, considers in huge populaces rely upon shockingly shortsighted and guileless information assortment strategies, for example, memory and self-announcing, which produce famously inconsistent information. Against this foundation commotion, nourishment look into has a difficult activity.

Is There A Quick Fix?

Sadly, not. Sensationalized features and often a hyperbolic portrayal of scientific information brings about the apparently unlimited debates about what – and how much – we ought to eat, further fueling our fixation on a "convenient solution" or marvel fix, which in itself is an endemic social issue.

For the reasons sketched out, the Sirtfood diet ought to be entrusted to the prevailing fashion heap – at any rate from a scientific point of view. In light of the proof we have, to recommend in any case is, best case scenario fake and even under the least favorable conditions deceiving and harming to the authentic points of general wellbeing procedure. The diet is probably not going to offer any profit to populaces confronting a scourge of diabetes, sneaking in the shadow of corpulence. As expressed plainly by others, uncommon diets don't work and dieting, all in all is certainly not a general wellbeing answer for social orders where the greater part of grown-ups are overweight.

By and by, the best technique is long haul conduct change joined with political and natural impact, focused on expanded physical movement and some type of cognizant command over what we eat. It is anything but a convenient solution, yet it will work.

A diet that underlines dull chocolate, red wine, kale, berries, and espresso? It either seems like the most ideal street to wellbeing and weight loss, or unrealistic.

However, pause, it shows signs of improvement: According to the makers of the Sirtfood Diet, these and other supposed "sirtfoods" are indicated to enact the components constrained by your body's characteristic "thin qualities" to assist you with consuming fat and get more fit.

Bragging a rundown flavorful nourishment, you presumably as of now love, and supported by reports that Adele utilized it to get in shape in the wake of having a child, the Sirtfood Diet sounds naturally engaging.

Be that as it may, not to destroy your chocolate-and-red-wine high here, yet the science doesn't really bolster the diet's greatest cases. Which isn't to say that eating sirtfoods is an ill-conceived notion . . . yet, similarly as with all diets that sound unrealistic, you should take a gander at this one with the genuine examination. This is what you have to think about what sirtfoods can and can't accomplish for you.

As a matter of first importance, what the hell is a sirtfood?

Manufactured by U.K. Sustenance experts Aidan Goggins and Glen Matten, the Sirtfood Diet highlights plant-based feeding stuff known as "sirtuin activators." Basically, you animate the SIRT1 quality encoded proteins that Goggins and Matten called "thin quality" when you look at the key arrangement fixtures.
SIRT1 and sirtuin proteins are accepted to assume a job in maturing and life span, which might be identified with the defensive impacts of calorie limitation.

The case behind the Sirtfood Diet is that sure nourishments can actuate these sirt-intervened pathways sans the limitation, and consequently "switch on your muscle to fat ratio's consuming forces, supercharge weight loss, and assist fight with offing infection."

Alongside red wine, dull chocolate, berries, espresso, and kale, sirtuin-advancing nourishments incorporate matcha green tea, additional virgin olive oil, pecans, parsley, red onions, soy, and turmeric (a.k.a. phenomenal flavors and go-to solid treats).

There's some science behind the cases of sirtfoods' advantages, yet it's exceptionally constrained and rather disputable.

The science on the sirt boondocks is still very new. There are contemplates investigating the SIRT1 quality's job in maturing and life span, in maturing related weight addition and maturing related illness, and in shielding the heart from aggravation brought about by a high-fat diet. In any case, the examination is restricted to work done in test tubes and on mice, which isn't adequate proof to state that sirtuin-boosting nourishments can have weight loss or against maturing capacities in an absolutely real human body.

Brooke Alpert, R.D., creator of The Sugar Detox, says there's an exploration to recommend that the weight-control advantages of sirtfoods may come to some degree from the polyphenol-cancer prevention agent resveratrol, often advertised as a component in red wine. "All things considered, it is difficult to devour enough red wine to get benefits," she says, noticing that she does much of the time recommend resveratrol enhancements to her customers.

Also, some nourishment specialists aren't psyched about the way the Sirtfood Diet plan works.

According to top dietitians who've evaluated the arrangement, the Sirtfood Diet is feeling the loss of some significant components for a sound, adjusted routine. Goggins and Matten's diet plan includes three stages: a couple of days at 1,000 calories for each day, made up of one sirtfood-overwhelming dinner and green squeezes; a couple of long periods of two sirtfood suppers and two squeezes per day, for an aggregate of 1,500 calories; and a fourteen-day support period of sirt-y suppers and juices.

Keri Gans, R.D., creator of The Small Change Diet, says that she's "not wild about anything that runs in stages." Usually, the shorter stages make a hardship organize, which just prompts gorging eventually. "When you're limiting, anybody will get in shape toward the beginning of a diet," she clarifies. "However, we can't continue that eating design long haul."

According to Lauren Blake, R.D., a dietitian at the Ohio State University Wexner Medical Center, when you're hydrating and squeezing a great deal without a huge amount of calorie consumption, weight loss is normal, "however it's an ordinarily liquid loss," she clarifies. So, while one may shed beats on the diet, it's probably going to be impermanent and might have nothing to do with sirtuins by any means.

The decision? Sirtfoods are incredible to have in your diet, however, they shouldn't be all you have.

There's positively no explanation you can't include some sirtfoods into your eating plan, says Alpert. "I think there are some truly fascinating things here, similar to the red wine, dull chocolate, matcha—I love these things," she says. "I love mentioning to individuals what to concentrate on rather than what to nix from their diet." If it tastes liberal and it's solid in little amounts, why not?

Gans says she's an enthusiast of a ton of the nourishments on the sirt list, including staples of the Mediterranean Diet—the highest quality level of scientifically-supported smart dieting—like olive oil, berries, and red wine. "I can get behind nourishments rich in polyphenols and cancer prevention agents," she says.

Blake concurs that there's bounty to adore about the nourishments remembered for the diet, particularly the stylish fixings like turmeric and matcha that vibe crisp and help make eating fun and intriguing. "I'm seeing a great deal of plant-based nourishments that truly sparkle, and are loaded up with phytonutrients," she says. "Those are calming, and bravo."

Be that as it may, all the nourishment specialists recommend balancing the diet with some lean protein and sound fats, for example, progressively nuts and seeds, avocado, and greasy fish like salmon. Stir up your plate of mixed greens game, as well, with more kinds of veggies, spinach, and romaine lettuce notwithstanding the kale and red onions. Main concern? A large portion of the sirtfoods are An OK to eat and solid for you, yet simply don't depend on the diet to enact any "thin quality" right now.

Chapter 5: Activation of Sirtuins

What makes the Sirtfood Diet so strong is their ability to turn to an ancient gene family that exists within each of us. The name for that gene family is sirtuin. Sirtuins are unique in that they orchestrate processes deep within our cells that affect things as important as our ability to burn fat, our vulnerability to disease — or not — and ultimately even our life span. The influence of sirtuins is so deep that they are now called "the chief metabolic regulators." Basically, what exactly someone who wants to lose a few pounds and live a long and happy life will want to be in control.

In recent years, sirtuins have, unsurprisingly, become the subject of intense scientific research. The first sirtuin was discovered in yeast back in 1984, and research really began in the course of the coming three decades when it was revealed that sirtuin activation increases life span, first in yeast, and then all the way up to mice.

Why the thrills?

Because the basic principles of cellular metabolism are almost identical from yeast to humans and everything in between. If you can manipulate something as tiny as budding yeast and see a benefit, then repeat it in higher organisms like mice, there is potential for the same benefits to be realized in humans.

That takes us to fast. Consistently, the lifelong limitation of food consumption has been shown to increase the life span of lower species and mammals. This remarkable finding is the basis for the practice of calories restriction for some people, where daily calorie consumption is decreased by 10 percent, as well as its popularized offshoot, intermittent fasting, which has become a common weight-loss diet, made famous by the likes of the 5:2 diet, or Fast Diet. Although we are still awaiting evidence of improved longevity for humans from these activities, there is evidence of benefits to what we could call "healthspan "— chronic diseases are declining, and fat is starting to melt away.

But let's be honest, no matter how significant the advantages, fasting week in, week out, is a grueling business that most of us don't want to sign up for. Even if we do, most of us are not willing to stick to this. Besides this, there are disadvantages to fasting, especially if we follow it for a long time. We listed in the introduction the side effects of hunger, irritability, fatigue, muscle loss, and slowing in metabolism. However, ongoing fasting schemes may also put us at risk of malnutrition, impacting our well-being due to a decreased intake of vital nutrients. Fasting schemes are often entirely inadequate for significant proportions of the population, such as infants, pregnant women, and most likely older adults. Although fasting has clearly proven benefits, it's not the magic bullet we'd like it to be. This makes us ask, is this really the way nature was supposed to make us slim and healthy? There's definitely a safer way out there.

Our breakthrough came when we discovered that the profound benefits of calorie restriction and fasting were mediated by triggering our ancient sirtuin genes 5. To better understand this, it might be beneficial to think of sirtuins as the guardians at the crossroads of energy status and longevity. Therefore, what they do is to respond to stress in the body.

When energy is in short supply, there is a rise in tension on our cells, just as we see in the caloric restriction. The sirtuins sensed this, and then turned on and transmitted a series of powerful signals that dramatically altered the behavior of cells. Sirtuins ramp up our metabolism, increase our muscle's efficiency, turn on fat burning, minimize inflammation, and repair any cell damage. Sirtuins, in turn, makes us fitter, leaner, and safer.

A Passion for Exercise?

It's not just caloric restriction and fasting that stimulates sirtuins; exercise also does. Sirtuins orchestrate the profound benefits of exercise much as in fasting. But while we are encouraged to participate in routine, moderate exercise for its multitude of benefits is recommended, it is not the means by which we are expected to focus our efforts on weight-loss. Research indicates that the human body has developed ways of adapting naturally and that the amount of energy that we use while exercising, which means that in order for exercise to be a successful weight-loss strategy, we need to devote considerable time and effort.

That grueling workout regimen is the way nature intended us to maintain a healthy weight loss; this is even more questionable in the light of studies, now indicating that too much exercise can be harmful — weakening our immune systems, damaging the heart and leading to an early death.

Enter Sirtfoods

So far, we have discovered that triggering our sirtuin genes is vital if we want to lose weight and be healthy. Fasting and exercise have been the two known ways of doing this up till now. Unfortunately, the amounts needed for successful weight loss come with their drawbacks, and for most of us, it's merely incompatible with how we live twenty-first-century lives. Luckily, there is a newly discovered, ground-breaking way to activate our sirtuin genes in the best way possible: sirtfood. As we'll soon know, these are the wonder foods that are particularly rich in specific natural plant chemicals that have the power to talk to our sirtuin genes and turn them on. In turn, they mimic the results of fasting and exercise and, in doing so, offer impressive benefits of burning fat, muscle building, and health-boosting that were once unachievable.

Dealing with the Fat

One of the dramatic results from our Sirtfood Diet pilot study was not just the amount of weight the participants lost, which was very impressive — it was the sort of weight loss that really excited us. What caught our attention was the fact that a lot of people lost weight without losing any muscle. It wasn't uncommon actually to see people growing muscle. That left us with an inevitable conclusion: fat merely melted away.

Achieving a significant fat loss normally requires a considerable sacrifice, either severely reducing calories or engaging in superhuman exercise levels or both. Contrary to that, our participants either maintained or lowered their level of exercise and did not even report feeling particularly hungry. In reality, some even struggled to eat all of the food they had been provided with.

How is it even possible? Only when we understand what happens to our fat cells when there is an increased sirtuin activity, then we begin to make sense of these incredible findings.

Lean Genes

Mice genetically engineered with high levels of SIRT1, the sirtuin gene that causes fat loss, are leaner and more metabolically active, 1 whereas mice without SIRT1 are fatter and have more metabolic disease. 2 When we look at humans, levels of SIRT1 have been found to be significantly lower in obese people's body fat than their healthy weight counts. This is because we get benefits on several levels by sirtuins, beginning at the very root of everything: the genes that regulate weight gain.

To understand this further, we need to look deeper into what is happening in our bodies, which is causing us to gain some weight.

Fat Busting

We will explain this in terms of a drug-ring in Hollywood. The streets flooding with drugs is our body flooding with fat. The drug pushers on the street corners are the source of the weight gain peddling reactions in our bodies. But in fact, it's just the low-level thugs. The true villain is behind it all, masterminding the entire operation, directing every deal that the peddlers make. This antagonist is referred to in our film as PPAR-π (peroxisome proliferator-activated receptor-ÿ). PPAR-ÿ orchestrates the cycle of fat accumulation by switching on the genes needed to start synthesizing and storing fat.6 To avoid fat proliferation, you need to cut supply. Stop PPAR-ÿ, and you avoid fat benefit effectively.

Enter our hero SIRT1, who rises to bring the villain down. With the villain locked up tightly, there is no one to pull the trigger and the whole fat-gain enterprise crumbles. With PPAR-π's operation halted, SIRT1 is turning its focus to "cleaning the streets." Not only is this achieved by shutting down fat production and storage, as we have shown, but it is also altering our metabolism so that we begin to clear the body of excess fat. Like any good crime-fighting hero, SIRT1 has a sidekick, a central regulator known as PGC-1α in our cells. This effectively stimulates the formation of what is known as mitochondria. These are the tiny factories of energy that exist within each of our cells — the power of the body. The more we have the mitochondria, the more we can generate the electricity. But as well as encouraging more mitochondria, PGC-1α also encourages them to burn fat as the fuel of choice to make the energy. Thus, fat accumulation is blocked on the one side, and fat burning on the other increases.

Wat or Bat

We have looked so far at the effects of SIRT1 on fat loss on a well-known fat form called white adipose tissue (WAT). This is the sort of fat that weight gain coincides with. It specializes in storage and expansion, is stubborn, and secretes a host of inflammatory chemicals that prevent fat burning and further fat accumulation, rendering us overweight and obese. That's why weight gain always starts slowly but can snowball so quickly.

But the sirtuin story has another intriguing angle, involving a lesser-known type of fat, brown adipose tissue (BAT), which behaves quite differently. BAT is advantageous to us in full contrast to white adipose tissue and needs to be used up. Brown adipose tissue helps us expend energy and has developed into mammals to allow them to dissipate large quantities of heat-shaped fat. This is known as a thermogenic influence and is vital to help small mammals survive in cold temperatures. Babies also contain substantial amounts of brown adipose tissue in humans, but it declines shortly after birth, leaving smaller amounts in adults.

This is where the activation of SIRT1 is doing something truly incredible. It changes genes in our white adipose tissue to transform and assume the properties of brown adipose tissue in what is called a "browning effect."[8] This means that our fat stores begin to act in a radically different way — instead of storing energy, they start mobilizing it to be disposed of.

Sirtuin activation, as we can see, has an effective direct action on fat cells, allowing the fat to melt away. But there, it's not over. The sirtuins also have a beneficial effect on the most important weight reduction hormones. Sirtuin activation increases insulin activity [9]. This helps to minimize insulin resistance — the failure of our cells to react to insulin adequately — which is heavily involved in weight gain. SIRT1 also enhances our thyroid hormones' release and activity,[10], which share several overlapping roles in boosting our metabolism and, ultimately, the rate at which we burn fat.

Chapter 6: Calorie Restriction and Lifespan

Fasting-based diets have become very popular over the past few years. In fact, studies show that by fasting - that is, with moderate daily calorie restriction or by practicing a more radical, but less frequent intermittent fast - you can expect to lose about six pounds in six months and substantially reduce the risk of contracting certain diseases.

When we fast, the reduction of energy reserves activates the so-called "lean gene", which causes several positive changes. The accumulation of fat stops and the body blocks normal growth processes and enters "survival" mode. Fats are burned faster and the genes that repair and rejuvenate cells are activated. As a result, we lose weight and increase our resistance to disease.

The mysteries of thinness

Many studies have looked at the genetic specificities of overweight or obese people, Sadaf Farooqi, professor at the University of Cambridge, has chosen to focus on those of thin people. For this research, Sadaf Farroqi and his team worked with 1,622 thin volunteers, and used data from 1,985 severely obese people and 10,433 people of normal weight. Their DNA was collected and they answered a questionnaire on their state of health and their lifestyle.

Slimming is linked to genetics

The DNA study confirmed the results of other studies: certain genes have a role in the risk of obesity and have allowed new discoveries to be made, in particular, that other genes seem to be involved in slimming. The researchers gathered the data collected to develop a genetic risk index. "As we imagined, we found that obese people have a higher genetic risk index than people with normal weight," said one of the study authors. Conversely, thin people have a lower genetic risk index. 74% of the slim people in the study had slim and healthy people in their genealogy.

Target these genes to avoid obesity

"It's easy to make hasty judgments and criticize people for their weight, but science shows that things are much more complex, says Sadaf Farooqi. We have much less control over our weight than we would like". He now wants to push his research to identify precisely which gene influences thinness, this could help put the weight of specific treatment strategies for overweight people.

All this, however, has a price. Lower energy intake leads to hunger, irritability, exhaustion and loss of muscle mass. And the problem is precisely this with fasting-based diets: when they are followed correctly, they work, but they make us feel so bad that we cannot respect them. The question, then, is the following: is it possible to obtain the same results without having to impose that drastic drop in calories and, therefore, without suffering the negative consequences?

At this point, we just have to present you the Sirt foods, a group of newly discovered foods. These genes are sirtuins. They became famous thanks to an important study conducted in 2003, during which scientists analyzed a particular substance, resveratrol, present in the peel of black grapes, red wine and yeast, which would produce the same effects of calorie restriction without need to decrease energy intake. The researchers then found that other substances in red wine had a similar effect, which would explain the benefits of consuming this drink and why those who consume it get less fat.

This naturally stimulated the search for other foods containing a high concentration of these nutrients, capable of producing such a beneficial effect on the body, and studies gradually discovered several. If some are almost unknown, such as lovage, a herb that is by now very little used in cooking, the great majority is represented by well-known and widely used food.

The super regulators of metabolism

After the discovery of 2003, enthusiasm for the benefits of Sirt food skyrocketed. Studies reveal that these foods don't just mimic the effects of calorie restriction.

They also act as super regulators of the entire metabolism and burn fat, increase muscle mass and improve the health of the cells. The world of medical research was close to the most important nutritional discovery of the century.

Unfortunately, a mistake was made: the pharmaceutical industry invested hundreds of millions of pounds in an attempt to turn Sirt foods into a sort of miracle pill, and the diet took a back seat. We do not share a similar pharmaceutical approach, which seeks (so far without result) to concentrate the benefits of these complex nutrients of plant origin into a single drug. Instead of waiting for the pharmaceutical industry to transform the nutrients of the foods we eat into a miraculous product (which may not work anyway), we find it more sensible to eat these substances in their natural form, that of foods, to take full advantage of them. This is the basis of our pilot experiment, with which we intended to create a diet containing the richest sources of Sirt foods and observe their effects.

A point in common among the healthiest diets in the world

During our studies, we have discovered that the best Sirt foods are regularly consumed by the peoples who boast the lowest incidence of disease and obesity in the world.

Among the Kuna Indians, in the American continent, who seem immune from hypertension and with very low levels of obesity, diabetes, cancer and early death thanks to the intake of cocoa, excellent Sirt food, as well as in Okinawa, Japan, where a Sirt food, dry physique and longevity go hand in hand. In India, the passion for spicy foods, especially turmeric, gives good results in the fight against cancer. And in the traditional Mediterranean diet, which the rest of the western world envies, obesity is contained, and chronic diseases are the exception, not the norm. Extra virgin olive oil, wild green leafy vegetables, dried fruit, berries, red wine, dates and aromatic herbs are all effective Sirt foods, and they are all present in the Mediterranean diet.

Although Sirt foods are not a mainstay of nutrition in England today, the situation was quite different in the past. They were a basic element, and if many have become rare and others have even disappeared, we will soon see that it is possible to reverse the course.
For the first time, researchers have just highlighted a genetic cause of pathological thinness, associated with a risk of high mortality.

These studies, which point to the role of excess genes in underweight people who have difficulty eating, are published on Wednesday by the British scientific journal Nature.

The study, which involved 100,000 people, was led by Philippe Froguel (Imperial College / London and Institute Pasteur de Lille / France) and the Swiss team of Jacques Beckmann (University of Lausanne).

A fragment of chromosome 16 is known to be sometimes subject to fluctuations in the number of copies of its genes. The vast majority of people have two copies of each gene in this part of the chromosome, one transmitted by the mother, the other by the father. But about one in 2,500 people has only one copy (an under-dosage) and one in 2,000 has three copies (overdose of genes).

The Franco-Anglo-Swiss team had discovered in 2010 that the presence of a hole (a single copy) in this fragment of chromosome 16 could explain 1% of severe obesity.

It now demonstrates that people with an excess of genetic material (a "duplication") and therefore having three copies of this part of chromosome 16 have significant, even extreme thinness. They are up to 20 times more likely to be underweight than the general population.

These excess genes, 28 in number, are probably "appetite genes", underlines Professor Froguel. Thus, in children, half of the carriers of this anomaly are underweight and find it very difficult to eat. They can suffer from a developmental disorder and weigh at 4 years the weight of a child of a year and a half, said AFP Professor Froguel.

The researchers identified 138 carriers of the anomaly out of the 100,000 people studied. "In a third of the cases, this mutation was absent in the parents and in the remaining two thirds it was hereditary," notes Professor Froguel.

Example of female thinness: 1m60 for 40 kg (BMI of the order of 15). In adults of both sexes, "at 40 kg mortality is as high as in people who weigh 100 kg," he says. This genetic defect affects longevity: "There is no old man" in identified carriers.

The excess or deficiency of certain genes on the same fragment of the chromosome leads to opposite pathological consequences, underweight or obesity. It remains to clarify the mechanisms involved.

Of the 100,000 people studied, the researchers identified 138 carriers of the anomaly. "In a third of the cases, this mutation was absent in the parents and in the remaining two thirds it was hereditary," notes Professor Froguel. The region of chromosome 16 concerned by this duplication phenomenon comprising 28 genes, another step will be to identify which one has an impact on appetite and weight. It could be a single gene or a combination of several of them. This work also demonstrates that if certain genes from the same genetic region are present in excess (three copies) or deficiently (only one copy), this can lead, by a "mirror effect", to reverse pathological consequences - here the underweight or obesity.

Chapter 7: Foods to Activate Sirtuins

We've learned so far that sirtuins are an ancient gene family with the ability to help us lose weight, create muscle, and keep us super healthy. It is well known that through dietary limitation, fasting, and exercise, sirtuins can be turned on, but there is another innovative way to do this: diet. We refer to the most potent foods to activate sirtuins as Sirtfoods.

Beyond antioxidants.

To better appreciate the benefits of Sirtfoods, we need to learn about foods like fruits and vegetables very differently, and why they are perfect for us. Despite tons of evidence demonstrating that diets high in fruits, vegetables, and processed products usually cut the risk of multiple infectious illnesses, including the greatest killers, heart failure, and cancer, there is no denying that they do. It has been put down to their rich nutritional content, such as vitamins, minerals, and antioxidants, which is perhaps the best wellness buzzword of the past decade.

Yet this is a very different story we are here to share.

The explanation Sirtfoods is so amazing for you has nothing to do with the nutrients that we all know so well and hear about so much. Yes, they're all important items you need to get out of your diet, but with Sirtfoods, there's something completely different, and very rare. What if we threw the entire way of thought on its head and said that the reason Sirtfoods is good for you is not that they nourish the body with vital nutrients, or have antioxidants to mop up the damaging effects of free radicals, but quite the opposite: because they are full of weak toxins? This could sound insane in a world where almost every alleged "superfood" is actively promoted based on its antioxidant content. But it's a groundbreaking concept, and one worth taking on.

Sirtfoods may be a new culinary innovation, but it's obvious that throughout history, diverse societies have enjoyed their benefits. As we are more acquainted with the top twenty Sirtfoods below, we can see how many have been valued for their medicinal properties since early history, and have also been considered sacred foods for their ability to impart vigor and well-being.

Yes, it now seems that published evidence of these Sirtfoods benefits goes back a long way to being the subject of the very first clinical trial ever conducted. He was documented in Daniel in the Bible more than 2,200 years ago, we and him. It was considered the best food possible of the day and was recommended to keep the young people alive and eventually join the monarch's service. And, when Daniel opposed this, a plant-only diet yielded a better outcome in only a couple of days.

Such benefits should usually never be expected from a diet of only plants, particularly increased muscle mass. This, of course, is because certain plants were incredibly rich sources of Sirtfood. With reports revealing that the typical plants eaten back then were identical to the Sirtfood-rich conventional Mediterranean diet, and findings remarkably close to our pilot experiment, one can't help wonder whether the Daniel study is the stuff of fable, or do we unwittingly have the solution to achieving the body and well-being we've all desired for over two millennia?

Chapter 8: Top 20 SIRT Foods

The sirtfood diet comprises of a variety of different foods. The most significant benefit of a sirtfood diet is the wide variety of different food spectrum which can be incorporated in our personalized diet plan. The sirtfood diet can also have coffee and wine, which is the most popular reason that many celebrities are following this diet plan. sirtfoods are the most common and most widely used foods in both the Western and Eastern worlds. To be very specific, sirtfoods are those which contain high levels of a chemical compound called polyphenol. This compound is not uniformly distributed in sirtfoods, but every sirtfood contains specific amounts of polyphenols. You must be thinking that why only polyphenols are being tackled here. The answer is straightforward yet very informative. Polyphenols are the compounds that are present naturally in sirtfood, and many types of research conducted on these foods have confirmed that these foods have the highest impacts when losing extra pounds of fats from the body. However, the most famous foods in the sirtfood diet are actually twenty in number, and a significant portion of a sirtfood diet comprises of these superfoods. The reason to stick this food on a more significant proportion of the sirtfood diet is the higher number of polyphenols present in these foods, which is essential to unlocking the sirtuin gene in the body. This gene is arguably the most critical gene to trigger many fat loss cycles in the human body.

The top twenty sirtfoods are:

1. Arugula

The critical factor is the nutritious benefits provided by this food, which is rich in very unique and rare benefits. It is an outstanding food that can be used in health promotion and anti-aging. It is also called a superfood. A vast scientific literature is dedicated to supporting this food. It contains high amounts of antioxidants, antifungal, antiviral, disinfectant, and protecting benefits. It is also essential in the reduction of cholesterol from the body and thus reduces the chances of atherosclerosis and heart attacks.

A word Ramayana is used in traditional Indian medicine, which is associated with the global benefits of arugula in the human body. Arugula is a natural coolant that can be a protective remedy during hot summers. It also has cooling effects on the liver and stomach.

2. Buckwheat:

Stomach acids, disturbed gut mobility and injured food canal (esophagus) cause heartburn, a condition that affects every human many times in their lives. Buckwheat prevents heartburn by improving the capacities of the stomach and colon as well as by healing the food canal. Our large and small intestines have bacteria called E. coli, which are friendly in nature and help in digesting the food. Buckwheat is helpful to E. coli and thus improves the medium inside the large and small intestine. That helps to prevent irritable bowel syndrome and Crohn's disease, conditions that affect the colon adversely. It can effectively treat the issues related to constipation due to high concentrations of fiber.

3. Capers

The importance of this root plant in traditional Chinese herbalism is well known. It is considered a great root to promote the self-healing capacity of the body and to maintain vital forces inside the body. Some western herbalists also used this root as the primary source of tonic, which is essential to promote natural immunity and vital capacities of the body. This root has some fantastic impacts on neural and endocrinal systems of the body. It can be a primary herbal remedy for patients with deficient immunity or those who are treated by chemotherapy and radiotherapy.

These benefits of the herb make it an herbal remedy of choice for cancer patients all over the world. It is a primary adaptive herbal remedy in oncology. Moreover, the use of astragalus is hazard-free and safe. It has a fantastic impact on bone marrow, and thus, it can easily promote immunity by producing more potent white blood cells that can be used in the war against the deadly pathogens like bacteria and viruses. It is very high in concentrations of polyphenols, which help in reducing body fats from the body.

4. Celery

Much like to buckwheat, celery is very important for our stomach and intestine. Stomach acids, disturbed gut mobility, and injured food canal (esophagus) cause heartburn, a condition that affects every human many times in their lives. Celery prevents heartburn by improving the capacities of the stomach and colon as well as by healing the food canal. Our large and small intestines have bacteria called E. coli, which are friendly in nature and help in digesting the food. Buckwheat is helpful to E. coli and thus improves the medium inside the large and small intestine. That helps to prevent irritable bowel syndrome and Crohn's disease, conditions that affect the colon adversely. It can effectively treat the issues related to constipation due to high concentrations of fiber.

5. Chilies

Chilis are used in both western and eastern foods and can be utilized to achieve higher metabolic rates because these are rich in capsicum.

Capsicum is a potent fat mobilizer that can be used to break adipose tissues into much simpler precursors called fatty acid. Its action is dual. When these free fatty acids reach in our blood, the action of capsicum in chilies is to increase the basal metabolic rate, which is highly essential to burn these extra fatty acids in the bloodstream and thus promoting a lean physique without extra fat.

6. Cocoa

Cocoa is very important for the brain. By improving overall health and through its antioxidant properties, cocoa can reduce the chances of dementia, Parkinsonism, and much other related pathology. Fatigue is another crucial aspect to be tackled here. Mental fatigue is related to the exhausting of the brain after prolonged functioning or reduced brain capacities, which can lead to general body pains and low self-esteem. By providing the nutritional supply to the brain, cocoa can help to prevent the mental as well as general fatigue.

7. Coffee

Coffee is the reason for the popularity of the sirtfood diet. This diet regime allows the intake of caffeine in the body so that it can help in breaking the adipose tissues into fatty acid. Coffee, especially caffeine anhydrous, is beneficial in the mobilization of fats. Moreover, coffee also helps in reducing the fatigue in the brain, and it helps in the promotion of mental alertness. It is the biggest cause that the sirtfood diet provides mental focus and alertness to its users, which is not provided in many other ordinary fat loss diet plans.

8. Extra virgin olive oil

Olive oil is the most used type of oil throughout the globe. Italian and French diets primarily include olive oils in the main course. Extra virgin olive oil is the lightest form of olive oil. It provides many polyunsaturated fatty acids, which are actually high-density lipids. These fatty acids are essential in the reduction of blood cholesterol levels as well as they are a vital energy source in the body. Olive oil is well-researched about its benefits on the brain and cardiac health, and honestly, this attempt is not sufficient to describe the benefits of olive oil.

9. Green tea

Green tea is one of the most used types of tea around the world because of its health benefits. Green tea is well-researched about its benefits on the brain and cardiac health, and honestly, this writing is not sufficient to describe the benefits of olive oil. Green tea has rich historical importance in Indian ayurvedic medicine as well as in traditional western medicine. It was widely used to promote attention, focus, long-term and short-term memory, and brainpower in both children and adults. It was also used as an effective tonic for the heart and vascular health. In some literature, it is also shown that it was also used in lung diseases.

10. Red wine

The first evidence of grapes was found in Egyptian culture, and they were cultivated at the bank of Neil River. The literature is not complete to build a consensus that grapes were used in Egyptian civilization, but it is clear that they were very fond of wine even they were the first one who introduced it. So, it can be possible that they did enjoy the taste of red grape wine. However, history shows that once the drink was introduced, it spread at a swift pace over different zones of the globe, much like we are observing it today. In 55 B.C. after the arrival of Roman in British waters, they found locals enjoying a traditional cider-like drink, which appealed to them too, and soon, it was being considered as one of their favorite beverages. So, this beverage, with small changes in the recipe, was introduced in the Roman Empire and then to Europe. It was the most popular drink of Germanic heritage, and they added it to the Normans. When Normans defeated the British Empire in the 9th century, they brought the word "wine" into the English dictionary.

In many other fat loss diets, wine is a prohibited drink, but the sirtfood diet is unique in this regard. The sirtfood diet allows the use of red grape wine, and even it is an essential part of the sirtfood diet because of many health benefits assured by red grape wine.

Other foods which mark the top twenty list of the sirtfood diet are:

1) **Garlic**
2) **Kale**
3) **Medjool dates**
4) **Parsley**
5) **Red endive**
6) **Red onion**
7) **Soy**
8) **Strawberries**
9) **Turmeric**
10) **Walnuts**

Chapter 9: The Potential Health and Weight Loss Benefits

Ecological factors significantly influence the destiny of living beings and sustenance is one of the most persuasive variables. These days life span is a significant objective of medicinal science and has consistently been a fabrication for the individual since antiquated occasions. Specifically, endeavors are planned for accomplishing effective maturing, to be specific a long life without genuine ailments, with a decent degree of physical and mental autonomy and satisfactory social connections.

Gathering information unmistakably exhibits that it is conceivable to impact the indications of maturing. Without a doubt, wholesome mediations can advance wellbeing and life span. A tribute must be given to Ancel Keys, who was the first to give strong logical proof about the job of sustenance in the wellbeing/sickness balance at the populace level, explicitly in connection to cardiovascular illness, still the main source of death overall. It is commonly valued that the sort of diet can significantly impact the quality and amount of life and the Mediterranean eating regimen is paradigmatic of an advantageous dietary example

The developing cognizance of the useful impacts of a particular dietary example on wellbeing and life span in the second 50% of the only remaining century produced a ground-breaking push toward structuring eats fewer carbs that could diminish the danger of constant maladies, subsequently bringing about solid maturing. Subsequently, during the 1990s the Dietary Approaches to Stop Hypertension (DASH) diet was contrived so as to assess whether it was conceivable to treat hypertension not pharmacologically. To be sure, the DASH diet was very like the Mediterranean Diet, being wealthy in foods grown from the ground, entire grains, and strands, while poor in creature-soaked fats and cholesterol. The awesome news leaving the investigation was that not exclusively did the DASH diet lower circulatory strain; however, it additionally diminished the danger of cardiovascular infection, type 2 diabetes, a few sorts of malignant growth, and other maturing related maladies To additionally improve the medical advantages of plant nourishment rich, creature fat-terrible eating routines, especially in hypercholesterolemic people, the Portfolio Diet was planned This eating regimen, other than being to a great extent veggie-lover, with just limited quantities of soaked fats, prescribes likewise a high admission of utilitarian nourishments, including thick filaments, plant stanols, soy proteins, and almonds. Curiously, members on the Portfolio Diet displayed a decrease of coronary illness chance related to lower plasma cholesterol and incendiary files in contrast with members on a sound, for the most part, vegan diet.

Nonetheless, additionally, the measure of ingested nourishment has been pulling in light of a legitimate concern for mainstream researchers as a potential modifier of the harmony among wellbeing and infection in a wide range of living species.

Specifically, calorie limitation (CR) has been exhibited to be a rising healthful intercession that animates the counter maturing instruments in the body.

In this way, the eating routine of the individuals living on the Japanese island of Okinawa has been widely broken down on the grounds that these islanders are notable for their life span and expanded wellbeing range, bringing about the best recurrence of centenarians on the planet.

Interestingly, the customary Okinawan diet came about to be fundamentally the same as the Mediterranean Diet and the DASH diet regarding nourishment types. Be that as it may, the vitality admission of Okinawans, at the hour of the underlying logical perceptions, was about 20% lower than the normal vitality admission of the Japanese, along these lines deciding an average state of CR.

In his most recent examination, showing up in the Aug8 print release of the diary Cell Metabolism, he saw what happens when the SIRT1 protein is absent from fat cells, which make up muscle versus fat.

At the point when putting on a high-fat eating regimen, mice coming up short on the protein began to create metabolic issues, for example, diabetes, much sooner than typical mice were given a high-fat eating routine.

"You've expelled one of the protections against metabolic decay, so on the off chance that you presently give them the trigger of a high-fat eating routine, they're considerably more delicate than the typical mouse."

The discovery raises the likelihood that medications that upgrade SIRT1 action may help ensure against weight connected illnesses. From that point forward, these proteins have been appeared to arrange an assortment of hormonal systems, administrative proteins, and different qualities, keeping cells alive and solid.

SIRT1 is a protein that expels acetyl bunches from different proteins, changing their movement. The potential focuses of this deacetylation are various, which is likely what gives SIRT1 its wide scope of defensive forces, Guarente says.

In the Cell Metabolism study, the specialists investigated the several qualities that were turned on in mice lacking SIRT1 yet encouraged a typical eating regimen and found that they were practically indistinguishable from those turned on in ordinary mice sustained a high-fat eating regimen.

This recommends in typical mice; improvement of the metabolic issue is a two-advance procedure. "The initial step is inactivation of SIRT1 by the high-fat eating routine, and the subsequent advance is all the terrible things that follow that," Guarente says. The scientists explored how this happens and found that in ordinary mice given a high-fat eating routine, the SIRT1 protein is cut by a compound called caspase-1, which is instigated by irritation. It's now realized that high-fat eating regimens can incite irritation, however, it's hazy precisely how that occurs, Guarente says. "What our examination says is that once you incite the fiery reaction, the outcome in the fat cells is that SIRT1 will be severed," he says.

That discovering "gives a pleasant sub-atomic system to see how fiery signals in fat tissue could prompt quick unhinging of metabolic tissue," says Anthony Suave, a partner teacher of pharmacology at Weill Cornell Medical College, who was not part of the exploration group.

Medications that focus on that incendiary procedure, just as medications that improve sirtuin action, may have some gainful remedial impact against heftiness related issues, Suave says.

Chapter 10: Empowering Yourself with Sirt Foods Building a Diet That Works

With the Sirtfood Diet, we've done something very special.

We've taken the foremost potent Sirtfoods on the earth and have woven them into a brand-new way of eating, the likes of which haven't been seen before. We've selected the "best of the best" from the healthiest diets ever known and from them created a world-beating diet.

The good news is, you don't need to suddenly adopt the normal diet of an Okinawan or be ready to cook like an Italian mamma. That's not only completely unrealistic but unnecessary on the Sirtfood Diet. Indeed, one thing which will strike you from the list of Sirtfoods is their familiarity. While you'll not currently be eating all the foods on the list, you presumably are consuming some.

So why are you not already losing weight?

The answer is found once we examine the various elements that the foremost cutting-edge nutritional science shows are needed for building a diet that works. It's about eating Sirtfoods within the right quantity, variety, and form. It's about complementing Sirtfood dishes with generous servings of protein than eating your meals at the simplest time of day. And it's about the liberty to eat the authentically tasty foods that you simply enjoy within the amounts you wish.

Hitting Your Quota

Right now, most of the people simply don't consume nearly enough Sirtfoods to elicit a potent fat-burning and health-boosting effect.

When researchers checked out the consumption of 5 key sirtuin-activating nutrients (quercetin, myricetin, kaempferol, luteolin, and apigenin) within the US diet, they found individual daily intakes to be a miserly 13 milligrams per day. In contrast, the typical Japanese intake was five times higher. Compare that with our Sirtfood Diet trial, where individuals were consuming many milligrams of sirtuin-activating nutrients a day.

What we are talking about maybe a total diet revolution where we increase our daily intake of sirtuin-activating nutrients by the maximum amount as fiftyfold. While this might sound daunting or impractical, it really isn't. By taking all our top Sirtfoods and putting them together during a way that's totally compatible together with your busy life, you can also easily and effectively reach the extent of intake needed to reap all the advantages.

The Power of Synergy

We believe it's better to consume a good range of those wonder nutrients within the sort of natural whole foods, where they coexist alongside the many other natural bioactive plant chemicals that act synergistically to spice up our health. We expect it's better to find out with nature, instead of against it. It's, for this reason, that point and time again supplements of isolated nutrients fail to point outlasting benefit, yet the exact same nutrient, when provided within the sort of whole food, does.

Curcumin is well established to be the key sirtuin-activating nutrient in turmeric, yet research shows that whole turmeric has better PPAR-γ activity for fighting fat loss and is simpler at inhibiting cancer and reducing blood glucose levels than curcumin in isolation. It's not difficult to ascertain why isolating one nutrient is nowhere near as effective as consuming it in its whole food form.

But what makes a dietary approach really special is once we begin to mix multiple Sirtfoods. For instance, by adding in quercetin-rich Sirtfoods, we enhance the bioavailability of resveratrol-containing foods even further. Not only this, but their actions complement one another. Both are fat busters, but there are nuances in how each of them achieves this. Resveratrol is extremely effective at helping to destroy existing fat cells, whereas quercetin excels in preventing new adipose cell formation. In combination they aim fat from each side, leading to a greater impact on fat loss than if we just ate large amounts of one food.

And this is often a pattern we see over and once again. Foods rich within the sirtuin activator apigenin improve the absorption of quercetin from food and enhance its activity. In turn, quercetin has been shown to synergize with the activity of epical catechin gallate (EGCG). And EGCG has been shown to find out synergistically with curcumin. Then it goes on. Not only are individual whole foods stronger than isolated nutrients, but by combining Sirtfoods we tap into an entire tapestry of health benefits that nature has weaved—so intricate, so refined, it's impossible to undertake to trump it.

Juicing and Food: Get the simplest of Both Worlds

Both juices and whole foods are integral to the Sirtfood Diet.

Here, we are talking about juices specifically made employing a juicer—blenders and smoothie makers (such because the NutriBullet) won't work. For many, this may seem counterintuitive, on the idea that when something is juiced the fiber is removed. Except for leafy greens, this is often exactly what we would like.

The fiber from food contains what are called non-extractable polyphenols (or NEPPs). These are polyphenols, including sirtuin activators that are attached to the fibrous a part of the food and are only released when weakened by our friendly gut bacteria. By removing the fiber, we don't get the NEPPs and lose out on their goodness. But importantly, the NEPP content varies dramatically counting on the sort of plant. The NEPP content of foods like fruit, cereals, and nuts is critical, and these should be eaten whole (in strawberries, NEPPs provide quite 50 percent of the polyphenols!). Except for leafy vegetables, the active ingredients within the Sirtfood juice, they're far lower despite an outsized bulk of fiber.

So, when it involves leafy greens, we get maximum bang for our buck by juicing them and removing the low-nutrient fiber, meaning we will use much greater volumes and achieve a super-concentrated hit of sirtuin-activating polyphenols. There is also another advantage of removing the fiber. Leafy greens contain a kind of fiber called insoluble fiber, which features a scrubbing action within the gastrointestinal system. But once we eat an excessive amount of it, a bit like if we over scrub something, it can irritate and damage our gut lining. Meaning leafy green–packed smoothies are going to be fiber overload for several people, potentially aggravating or may be causing IBS (irritable bowel syndrome) and hindering our absorption of nutrients.

Having a number of your Sirtfoods in juice form also can have big advantages when it involves absorbing their goodness. For instance, one among the ingredients we include within the green juice is matcha tea. Once we consume the sirtuin activator EGCG, found in high levels in tea, in drink form without food, its absorption is quite 65 percent higher. We also find it interesting to notice that once we ran blood tests on our own clients, switching from smoothies to green juices caused dramatic increases in their levels of other essential nutrients like magnesium and vitamin Bc.

The crux of it all is that to actually get those sirtuin genes to ring for dramatic weight loss and health, we'd like to create a diet that mixes both juices and whole foods for max benefit.

Go Big on Taste
A fundamental problem with conventional dieting is that it typically takes for a miserable dining experience. It drains all drop of delight from food, leaving us feeling dissatisfied.

But for us, it's essential that you simply maintain the enjoyment of food within the pursuit of a healthy weight. That's why we were delighted once we realized that Sirtfoods, also because the foods that enhance their activities like protein and omega-3 food sources, are primed to satisfy our desire for taste. It's the last word win-win: the Sirtfood Diet boosts our health and tastes great.

Let's take a step back to ascertain how this works. Our taste buds determine how tasty we discover our food, and the way satisfied we are from eating it. This is often done through seven major taste receptors.

Over countless generations, humans have evolved to hunt out the tastes that stimulate these receptors so as to realize maximum nourishment from our diet. The higher a food stimulates these taste receptors, the more satisfaction we get from a meal. And within the Sirtfood Diet, we have got the last word menu for happy taste buds because it offers maximum stimulation across all taste receptors. To summarize these tastes and therefore the foods you'll be eating on the diet that satisfies them: the seven major taste sensations are sweet (strawberries, dates); salty (celery, fish); sour (strawberries); bitter (cocoa, kale, endive, extra virgin vegetable oil, green tea); pungent (chilies, garlic, extra virgin olive oil); astringent (green tea, red wine); and umami (soy, fish, meat).

Crucially, what we've discovered is that the greater the sirtuin-activating properties of food, the more powerful y it stimulates those taste centers, and therefore the more gratification we get from the food we eat. Importantly, it also means we satisfy our appetite quicker, and our desire to eat more is reduced accordingly. This is often a key reason why those that follow a Sirtfood-rich diet are pleasantly fuller more quickly.

For example, natural cocoa features a striking, appealing bitter taste, but removes the sirtuin-activating flavanols with aggressive industrial food-processing techniques and that we are left with mass-produced, bland, and characterless cocoa that's want to make highly sugared chocolate confectionery. By now, the health benefits have vanished.

The same principle applies to vegetable oil. Consumed in its minimally processed form—extra virgin—it features a powerful and distinct flavor, with an invigorating kick that will be felt at the rear of the throat. Yet refined and processed vegetable oil loses all character, is mild and bland, and carries no such kick. Similarly, hot chilies boast much greater sirtuin-activating credentials than the milder varieties, and wild strawberries are much tastier than farmed ones thanks to a richer content of sirtuin-activating nutrients.

Not only this, but we also find that individual Sirtfoods can trigger multiple taste receptors: tea is both bitter and astringent, and strawberries have a mixture of sweet and sour flavors.

Initially, some palates won't be familiar with certain of those flavors—so much of our modern food is barren of both nutrients and true taste—but you'll be amazed how quickly you acquire a love for them. After all, humans evolved to hunt out a diet rich in Sirtfoods, alongside healthful protein and omega-3 fatty acids, to satisfy the essential desires of our appetite and, in turn, our health. This evolutionary process occurred over millennia, without us knowing the explanations, yet it ensured we got maximum to enjoy consuming these foods.

Chapter 11: How to Follow the Sirt Diet

Phase One and Phase Two?

The Sirtfood diet consists of two phases. I have to warn you, the first week of food is the hardest part. And you need to focus on the end of the first week, especially the early three days. Don't worry; the long-term plan is easy to follow and maintain.

The First Step

This level is divided into two levels (days 1, 2 and 3 / days 4, 5, 6 and 7).

For days 1, 2 and 3, dieters should consume two green juices per day (including green tea, parsley, lemon, celery, arugula and kale) and only one meal. You should limit your intake to just 1,000 calories a day.

I call this the detox/quick/juice phase, and it is generally intended for those who want to accelerate weight loss. The key, of course, is that every juice or meal contains Sirtfood ingredients.

To cope with the first three days, just keep an eye on the goal: lighter weight and a healthier body. And don't worry, the green juice is not that bad (I like these green juices). They also have a sumptuous dinner and can even make dark chocolates to appease your treats.

The second phase

Congratulations! You have completed the first week of "Hardcore".

The second phase is the simplest and consists of including sirtuin-based foods in your diet or your daily meals. You can call this the "maintenance phase".
In this way, your body goes through the stage of burning fat and building muscle, as well as strengthening your immune system and your general health.
In this phase, you can now eat three balanced meals with Sirtfood plus one green juice per day.

There is no "diet", but the choice of healthier alternatives by adding Sirtfood to each meal as often as possible.

Then, I will provide delicious cooking recipes with Sirtfood to give you an idea of the excitement and health of this diet trip.

What are sirtuins?

Sirtuins, or SIRT for short, belong to the family of proteins that regulate cell health, including homeostasis. Hemostasis is the process by which the body maintains its stability and adjusts the conditions most conducive to its survival.

The SIRT family of proteins includes seven members (SIRT1-7). The yeast mute information regulator SIR2 is the founding member of the SIRT family of proteins, which controls chromatin, DNA recombination and gene expression.

Among the seven mammalian SIRTs, SIRT1, SIRT2 and SIRT3 have a deacetylase capacity. The other remaining SIRTs (SIRT4, SIRT5, SIRT6 and SIRT7) have weak or undetectable deacetylate activity. SIRT1-7 differ in their function and location.

SIRT1 is located in the cytosol and in the cell nucleus, where it fulfils its cell life function. It is involved in glucose metabolism, neurodegeneration, differentiation, control of gene expression, ageing, cell death and tumor development. SIRT2 is in the cytosol and catalyzes the deacetylation of alpha-tubulin (Lys40), H3lys56, FOXO1, H4lys16 and FOXO3a. Also, it is involved in the regulation of gene expression, tubulin acetylation, tubulin acetylation, cell cycle regulation, response to DNA damage, cancer and neurodegeneration...

Localization of SIRT3 on the inner membrane of the mitochondria with long-chain substrates acyl-CoA dehydrogenase (LCDA), acetyl-CoA synthetase 2 (ACS2), 2,3-hydroxy-3-methyl glutaryl CoA synthetase 2 (HMGCS2), ornithine Transcarbamoyl transferase (OTC), glutamate dehydrogenase (GDH), cycle-Philip D, superoxide dismutase 2 (SOD2), Isocitrate dehydrogenase 2 (IDH2), many components of the respiratory chain complexes of mitochondria and Ku70. It is responsible for the production of mitochondrial ATP, the oxidation of fatty acids and the regulation of mitochondrial protein. It also controls caloric restriction and cellular response to oxidative stress by activating SOD2 and IDH2, which in turn reduces oxidized reactive oxygen species (ROS) and glutathione. It is also involved in the suppression of tumors and cell death, which has a positive impact on genomic stability. SIRT4 is in the mitochondrial matrix. It is engaged in the ribosylation of ADP and inhibition of GHD using NAD +.

SIRT5, it is also found in the mitochondrial matrix and contains a decarboxylase dependent on NAD + and the succinyls activity in CPS1.

SIRT6, which acts as a deacetylase and ADP ribosyltransferase, is necessary for telomeric functions, hemostasis of metabolism, DNA repair and genome stability.

SIRT7 is mainly a nucleolar protein which regulates the transcription of ribosomal genes by interaction with RNA polymerase 1. SIRT7 has a high selectivity for H3lys18 and a deacetylase dependent on NAD +. When SIRT7 is deacetylated, we must suppress the genes involved in cell anchoring and inhibit contact, thus promoting the malignant phenotype of tumor cells. As well as desuccinylase activity in CPS1. SIRT6, which acts as a deacetylase and ADP ribosyltransferase, is necessary for the functions of telomeres, hemostasis of metabolism, DNA repair and genome stability. SIRT7 is mainly a nucleolar protein which regulates the transcription of ribosomal genes by interaction with RNA polymerase 1.

SIRT7 has a high selectivity for H3lys18 and a deacetylase dependent on NAD +. When SIRT7 is deacetylated, we need to suppress the genes involved in cell anchoring and inhibit contact, thus promoting the malignant phenotype of tumor cells. As well as the desuccinylase activity in CPS1. SIRT6, which acts as a deacetylase and ADP ribosyltransferase, is necessary for telomeric functions, hemostasis of metabolism, DNA repair and genome stability. SIRT7 is mainly a nucleolar protein, which regulates the transcription of ribosomal genes by interaction with RNA polymerase 1. SIRT7 has a high selectivity for H3lys18 and a deacetylase dependent on NAD +. When SIRT7 is deacetylated, we must suppress the genes involved in cell anchoring and inhibit contact, thus promoting the malignant phenotype of tumor cells.

Genome stability. SIRT7 is mainly a nucleolar protein which regulates the transcription of ribosomal genes by interaction with RNA polymerase 1. SIRT7 has a high selectivity for H3lys18 and a deacetylase dependent on NAD +. When SIRT7 is deacetylated, we need to suppress the genes involved in cell anchoring and inhibit contact, thus promoting the malignant phenotype of tumor cells.

Genome stability. SIRT7 is mainly a nucleolar protein which regulates the transcription of ribosomal genes by interaction with RNA polymerase 1. SIRT7 has a high selectivity for H3lys18 and a deacetylase dependent on NAD +. When SIRT7 is deacetylated, we need to suppress the genes involved in cell anchoring and inhibit contact, thus promoting the malignant phenotype of tumor cells.

The science of sirt food
The sirt diet cannot be classified as low in carbohydrates or low in fat. This diet is very different from its many predecessors and at the same time advocates many of the same

things: eating fresh plant foods. As the name suggests, it is a diet based on sirtuins. But what are sirtuins, and why have you never heard of them?

There are seven Sirtuin proteins: SIRT-1 to SIRT-7a. They can be found in all cells and the cells of all animals on the planet. Sirtuins are found in almost all living organisms and nearly all parts of the cell and control what happens. The supplement company Elysium Health compares body cells to an office with sirtuins, which act as CEOs and help cells respond to internal and external changes. They regulate what is done when it is done and who does it.

Of the seven sirtuins, one acts in the cytoplasm of your cell, three in the mitochondria of the cell and three in the cell nucleus. They are busy, but they mainly eliminate acetyl groups from other proteins. These acetyl groups indicate that the protein to which they are attached is available to perform its function. The sirtuins remove the available flag and prepare the protein for use. Sirtuins seem quite crucial for the normal functioning of your body. Why have you never heard of it?

The first sirtuin discovered was SIR2, a gene found in the 1970s which controlled fruit flies' ability to mate. It wasn't until the 1990s when scientists discovered other similar proteins in nearly all life forms. Each organism had a different amount of sirtuins: one has bacteria and five has yeast. Mice experiments show that they have seven, the same number as humans.

Sirtuins have proved to prolong the yeasts and mice's life. So far, there is no evidence of the same effect in humans, but in almost all forms of life these sirtuins are present, and many scientists hope that organisms as distant as yeast and mice will have the same effect as sirtuins. Activation may be extended to humans, too.

In addition to sirtuins, our body needs another substance called.
Nicotinamide adenine dinucleotide for cells to function correctly. Elysium (see above) compares this substance to the money a business needs to keep it going. Like any CEO, a sirtuin can only manage the business properly if there is sufficient cash flow. NAD + was first discovered in 1906. You get your diet from NAD + from your diet by eating foods made from the building blocks of NAD +.

Chapter 12: Succeeding with Phase One

This is the period of hyper-success, where you will take a massive move in creating a slimmer, leaner body. Follow our easy step-by-step directions and use the delicious recipes you'll find. We also have a meat-free version in addition to our regular seven-day schedule, which is suitable for vegetarians and vegans alike. Feel free to go along with whatever you want.

What to Expect
You'll enjoy the full benefits of our clinically proven strategy of dropping 7 pounds in seven days during Phase 1. Yet note that involves adding strength, so don't hang up simply with the percentages on the scales. Nor should you become used to measuring yourself every day. In reality, in the last few days of Phase 1, we often see the scales rising due to muscle growth, although waistlines continue to shrink. So, we want you to look at the charts, but not be controlled by them. Find out how you feel inside the mirror, if your clothes fit, or if you need to push a knot on your belt. These are all perfect measures of the underlying shifts in your body composition.

Be mindful of other improvements, too, such as wellbeing, energy levels, and how smooth the skin is. In a local pharmacy, you can even get tests of your general cardiovascular and metabolic wellbeing to see improvements in factors like your blood pressure, blood sugar levels, and blood fats like cholesterol and triglycerides. Also, weight loss aside, incorporating Sirtfoods into your diet is a big step in making your cells fitter and more disease prone, setting you up for an extraordinary balanced lifetime.

How to Follow Phase 1
We will lead you through the full seven-day program one day at a time to make Phase 1 as plain sailing as possible, including the lowdown on the Sirtfood green juice and easy-to-follow, delicious recipes every step of the way.

This phase of Sirtfood Diet has two different stages:

Days 1 to 3 are the most important and you can eat up to a limit of 1000 calories every day during this time, consisting of:

- ➢ Three times Sirtfood green juices
- ➢ One main course

Days 4 to 7 will see the daily intake of food rise to a maximum of 1,500 calories, composed of:

- ➢ Two times Sirtfood green juices

> Two main courses

There are very few laws with which to obey the diet. Mostly, for lasting progress, it's about incorporating it into the lifestyle and around everyday life. But here are a few easy but big impact tips to get the best result:

1. Take a Good Juicer
Juicing is an essential aspect of the Sirtfood Diet, and a juicer is one of the best healthcare purchases you can make. Although price should be the determining factor, certain juicers are more effective at extracting the juice from green leafy vegetables and herbs, with the Breville brand among the best juicers we've tested.

2. Start Preparation
One thing is clear from the multitude of feedback we've had: those who planned ahead of time were the most successful. Get to know the products and techniques, and stock up on what's essential. You'll be amazed at how natural the whole cycle is, with everything planned and ready.

3. Save your Important Time
When time is tight, dress cleverly. Meals can be made the other night. Juices can be produced in bulk and stored in the refrigerator for up to three days (or longer in the freezer) until their sirtuin-activating nutrient levels begin to fall. Only shield it from light, and only add when you're able to eat it in the match.

4. Eat Early
Eating early in the day is healthier, and hopefully, meals and drinks should not be consumed after 7 p.m. But the plan is primarily designed to fit the lifestyle, and late eaters always enjoy great benefits.

5. Space Out the Juices
These should be taken at least one hour before or two hours after a meal to maximize the digestion of the green juices and dispersed throughout the day, rather than making them very close together.

6. Eat till You Feel Satisfied
Sirtfood can have dramatic effects on appetite, and some individuals will be satisfied before their meals are over. Hear your body and feed until you're full, instead of forcing down all the calories. Because Okinawans have existed for a long time, it states, "Feed before 80 percent full."

7. Enjoy the Diet
Don't get caught up on the end goal but keep aware of the road instead. This lifestyle is about enjoying food in all its glory, for its health benefits but also for the fun and pleasure it offers. Research shows that we are far more likely to succeed if we maintain our eyes focused on the road rather than the final destination.

Drinks
As well as the recommended daily portions of green beverages, other drinks can be easy drinking in Phase 1. Non-calorie beverages, usually regular juice, black coffee, and green tea. If your usual tastes are for black or herbal teas, do not hesitate to include these too. Fruit juices and soft drinks are left behind.
Alternatively, try adding a few sliced strawberries to still or sparkling water to make your Sirtfood-infused health drink, if you want to spice things up. Hold it for a few hours in the fridge, and you will have a surprisingly cooling option to soft drinks and juices.

One aspect that you have to be aware of is that we don't suggest abrupt, significant changes to your daily use of coffee. Symptoms of caffeine withdrawal can make you feel bad for a few days; similarly, significant increases can be painful for those particularly sensitive to caffeine results. They also recommend drinking coffee without adding milk, because some researchers have found that adding milk will decrease the absorption of the beneficial sirtuin-activating nutrients. The same has been observed with green tea but incorporating any lemon juice increases the absorption of its sirtuin-activating nutrients.

Note that this is the period of hyper-success, and while you should be comforted by the knowledge that it is only for a week, you need to be a little more careful. We have alcohol for this week, in the form of red wine but only as a cooking component.

The Sirtfoods Green Juices
The green juice is an essential part of the Sirtfood Diet's Phase 1 program. All the ingredients are strong Sirtfoods, and in every juice, you get a potent mixture of natural compounds like apigenin, kaempferol, luteolin, quercetin, and EGCG that function together to turn on your sirtuin genes and encourage fat loss. To that, we have attached lemon, as it has been shown that its natural acidity prevents, stabilizes, and improves the absorption of the sirtuin-activating nutrients. We added a touch of apple and ginger to taste too. But both of these are available. Nevertheless, several people find that they take the apple out entirely once they are used to the flavor of the fruit.

Sirtfood Green Juices (SERVES 1)

- Two handfuls (about two and a half ounces) kale
- A handful (one ounce or 30g) arugula
- A small handful (about one-fourth ounce or 5g) parsley leaves
- Two to three large celery stalks (five and a half ounces or 150g), including leaves
- Half medium green apple
- Half - to One-inch (1 to 2.5 cm) piece of fresh ginger
- Juice of a half lemon
- Half teaspoon matcha powder*

*Days 1 to 3 of Phase 1: added only to the first two juices of the day
*Days 4 to 7 of Phase 1: added to both juices

Remember that while we weighted all the amounts precisely as described in our pilot experiment, our experience is that a handful of measures work exceptionally well. In reality, they are the best tailoring the number of nutrients to the body size of a person. More significant people tend to have more massive paws, and thus get a proportionally higher volume of Sirtfood nutrients to suit their body size and vice versa for smaller people.

- Bring together the greens (kale, arugula, and parsley), and blend them. We consider juicers may vary in their efficacy when juicing leafy vegetables, and you may need to re-juice the remains before going on to the other ingredients. The goal is to end up with around 2 ounces of material, or about 1/4 cup (50ml) of green juice.
- Now, blend the Celery, apple, and ginger.
- You should cut the lemon and also bring it through the juicer, but we find it much easier to push the lemon into the juice by hand. You should have about 1 cup (250ml) of juice in total by this point, perhaps somewhat more.
- It's only when you extract the juice and are ready to serve that you add the matcha. In a bowl, pour a tiny amount of juice, then add the matcha, and mix vigorously with a fork or whisk. In the first two beverages of the day, we only use matcha, because it includes small amounts of caffeine (the same quality as a regular teacup). When wasted late, it can keep you awake with those not used to it.
- After the matcha is resolved, add the juice that left. Give it a final blend, and the juice is ready to drink. Easy to top up with plain water, as you like.

Chapter 13: Research Your Goal in Phase Two

Congratulations on completing Sirtfood Diet Step 1! You will already see amazing results with a weight loss and not only look slimmer and more toned but also feel revitalized and re-energized.

So, now what?

Having seen these often-remarkable transformations firsthand ourselves, we know how much you're going to want to see even better results, not just preserve all those benefits. Sirtfoods are, after all, designed to eat for life. The problem is how you adapt what you did in Phase 1 into your normal dietary routine. That's exactly what prompted us to develop a fourteen-day maintenance plan designed to help you make the transition from Phase 1 to your more usual dietary routine, thus helping to maintain and expand the Sirtfood Diet's benevolence.

What to Expect
You should maintain your weight-loss results during Phase 2, and continue to lose weight gradually.

Also, the one striking thing we've found with the Sirtfood Diet is that most or all of the weight people lose is from fat and that many actually put some muscle in.
So, we would like to remind you again not to measure your success solely on the scale by the numbers. Look in the mirror to see if you look leaner and more toned, see how your clothes are tingling, and lap up the compliments you're going to get from others.

Remember also that as the weight loss continues, so will the health benefits increase. By following the 14-day maintenance plan, you are really starting to lay the foundations for a lifelong health future.

How to Follow Phase 2
The key to success in this process is keeping your diet filled with Sirtfoods. To make it as simple as possible, we have prepared a seven-day menu plan for you to follow, including delicious family-friendly recipes, filled with Sirtfoods every day to the rafters (although see page 149 for children's advice). All you need to do is repeat the Seven Day Plan twice to complete Phase 2's fourteen days.

On each of the fourteen days, your diet will consist of:

• 3 x balanced sirtfood-rich meals

- 1 x sirtfood green juice
- 1 to 2 x optional snacks Sirtfood bite snacks

Once again, when you have to consume these, there are no rigid rules. Be flexible throughout your day, and t them. Two simple thumb rules are: • Have your green juice either in the morning, at least 30 minutes before breakfast, or in the middle of the morning. • Do your hardest to eat your dinner by 7 p.m.

Portion SIZES

During Phase 2, our attention is not on calorie counting. For the average person, this is not a practical approach or even a successful one over the long term.

Alternatively, we concentrate on small servings, really well-balanced meals, and, most importantly, filling up on Sirtfoods so that you can continue to enjoy their fat burning and health-promoting effects.

We've also designed the meals in the plan to make them satiate, making you feel satisfied for longer. That, combined with Sirtfoods' natural appetite-regulating effects, means you're not going to spend in 14 days feeling hungry, but rather happily satisfied, well-fed, and extremely well-fed.

Just like in Phase 1, remember to listen and be guided by your appetite. If you make meals according to our instructions, and you are comfortably full before you have a meal, then stop eating is perfectly fine!

What to Drink

In phase 2, you can need to have one green juice per day. This is to keep you top with high Sirtfoods levels.

Just as in Phase 1, during Phase 2, you can freely ingest other fluids. Our favorite beverages include remaining plain water, homemade flavored beer, coffee, and green tea. If black or white tea is your predilection, feel free to enjoy it. The same goes for herbal teas. The best news is that during Phase 2, you can enjoy the occasional glass of red wine. Because of its sirtuin-activating polyphenols content, especially resveratrol and piceatannol, red wine is a sirt food which makes it by far the best alcoholic beverage choice. But, with alcohol itself having adverse effects on our fat cells, moderation is still best and we recommend that you limit your intake for two or three days a week to one glass of red wine with a meal during Phase 2.

Chapter 14: How to Continue Managing Your Weight Returning to Three Meals

You ate only one or two meals a day during Phase 1, which gave you plenty of leisure time to eat your meals. As we are now returning to a more usual schedule and the time-tested practice of three meals a day, thinking about breakfast is a good time.

Eating a healthy breakfast will make us ready for the day and will increase our strength and focus. Eating earlier, in terms of metabolism, keeps our blood sugar and fat levels in check. Several studies have borne out that breakfast is a good thing, typically showing people who regularly eat breakfast are less likely to get overweight.

That is because of our internal body clocks. Our bodies are expecting us to eat early in anticipation of when we will be most busy and need food. Yet as many as a thirds of us will miss breakfasts on any given day. It's a classic symptom of our busy modern life, and the impression is there's simply not enough time to eat well. But as you will see, nothing could be further from the truth with the nifty breakfasts that we have laid out here for you. Whether it's the Sirtfood smoothie that can be drunk on the go, the premade Sirt muesli or the fast and easy Sirtfood scrambled eggs/tofu, finding those extra few minutes in the morning, will yield rewards not only for your day but for your weight and health over the longer term.

With Sirtfoods working to overcharge our energy levels, there's, even more, to gain from getting a hit from them early in the morning to start your day. This is done not only by eating a Sirtfood-rich meal but also by consuming the green juice, which we suggest you have either first thing in the morning — at least thirty minutes before a meal — or midmorning. We get plenty of accounts from our own clinical experience of people who drink their green juice first thing and don't feel hungry for a few hours afterwards. If this is the impact, it has on you, waiting a few hours before getting breakfast is perfectly fine. Only don't miss this one.

Alternatively, with a good meal, you can kick off your day, then wait two or three hours to get the green juice. Be flexible, and simply go for something that works for you.

Sirtfood Bites

When it comes to snacking, you should take it, or leave it. So much debate has been raised about whether eating regular, smaller meals is better for weight loss, or just sticking to three healthy meals a day. The fact is, that's just not important.

The way we've designed the maintenance menu for you means you're going to eat three well-balanced Sirtfood-rich meals a day, and you might not need a snack, either. But maybe you've been busy with working out or dashing with the kids, and you need something to tide you to the following meal. And if that "little thing" will give you a whammy of Sirtfood nutrients and delicious taste, then it's happy days. That's why we developed our "Sirtfood bites." These smart little treats are a truly guilt-free treat made entirely from sirtfoods: almonds, walnuts, chocolate, extra virgin olive oil, and turmeric. We recommend eating one, or a maximum of two, every day for the days that you need them.

"Sirtifying" Your Meals

We've noticed that inclusion, not exclusion is the only healthy diet. But true success goes beyond this — the diet has to be consistent with living in modern times. Whether it's the ease of meeting our hectic life's demands or fitting in with our position as the bon vivant at dinner parties, the way we eat should be trouble-free. You will enjoy your svelte body and radiant glow, rather than thinking about the demands and restrictions of kooky foods.

What makes Sirtfoods so fantastic is that they are very available, familiar, and easy to include in your diet. Here, as you cross the gap between step 1 and routine eating, you can lay the groundwork for a new, enhanced lifelong eating strategy.

The main idea is what we call your meals, "Sirtifying." This is where we take popular dishes, including several classic classics, and we keep all the great taste with some clever swaps and easy Sirtfood inclusions but add a lot of goodness to that. You'll see just how easily this is done during Phase 2.

Examples include our delicious smoothie Sirtfood for the perfect on-the-go breakfast in a time-consuming environment and the easy move from wheat to buckwheat to add extra flavor and zip to the much-loved pasta comfort food.

Meanwhile, classic, famous dishes such as chili con carne and curry don't even need much improvement, with Sirtfood bonanzas offering traditional recipes. And who has said that fast food means bad food? Once you make it yourself, we combine the authentic, vivid flavors of a pizza and remove the shame. There's no need to say goodbye to indulgence either, as our smothered pancakes with berries and dark chocolate sauce have proven. It's not even a dessert, it's breakfast, and for you it's perfect. Easy changes: you keep eating the foods that you enjoy when maintaining a healthy weight and wellbeing. And that is Sirtfoods, the dietary revolution.

Cooking for More

To support this, we are now entering a stage called "Sirtfoods for All," where the recipes begin to appeal to more than one mouth. Whether it's for family or friends, the new recipes for dinner, as well as the Sirtfood-packed soup that we introduce in this process, are planned with four in mind. And why not take advantage of cooking batch meals to freeze for those already cooking for one or two to have meals ready for the coming week?

Q&A

You should have found responses to most of your questions about the Sirt diet in the pages here.

However, I will try to find to answer any residual questions you might have so that you can begin your trip to success with more confidence.

Is Sirtfood healthy for children?

Children should avoid wine, coffee, and other highly caffeinated foods, such as Matcha. On the other hand, children can enjoy sirtuin-rich foods such as cabbage, eggplant, blueberries, and dates with their regular diet. Yet, while children can enjoy most sirtuin-rich foods, that is not the same as to say that they can practice the Sirt diet.

This diet plan is not intended for children, and it does not fit the needs of their growing bodies.

Practicing this diet plan could not only negatively affect them physically, but it could injury their mental health for years to come.
Anybody can develop an eating disorder, but it is particularly true for children.

If you want your child to eat healthily, ensure they eat a wide range of foods, as suggested by their doctor, and you can simply include plenty of sirtuin-rich foods into what they are already eating.

Put the focus on eating healthfully and not losing weight. Even if your child's doctor does want them to lose weight, you don't need to make the child aware of this fact. You can help guide them along with a healthy lifestyle, coaching them on how to eat well and stay active over sports and play, and the weight will come off naturally.

For similar reasons, you can include sirtfoods in a balanced diet while pregnant, but you should avoid an active Sirt diet when you are pregnant.

It doesn't contain the number of requirements for either a pregnant woman or a growing baby.

Save the diet for after you have delivered a healthy baby, and both you and your child will be healthy and happy.

Can I Exercise During Stage One?
If you are used to doing yoga and a spin class a few times a week, keep it up! If you are used to running a few miles a day, have at it! Do what you and your body are comfortable with, and as your doctor advises, and you should be fine
I'm Tinny. Can I Follow the Diet? Whether or not you can follow the first phase of the Sirt diet will depend just how thin you already are. While a person who is overweight or well within a healthy weight can practice the first phase, nobody who is clinically underweight should.

You can know if you are underweighting by calculating your Body Mass Index, or BMI. There are plenty of BMI calculators online, and if yours is at nineteen points or below, you should avoid the first stage of the diet.

It is always a good idea to ask your doctor if it is safe for you to lose weight, and if the Sirt diet is safe for your condition. While the Sirt diet is generally safe for people with certain illnesses, it may not be the case. While it is understandable to desire to be even more thin, even if you already are thin, pushing yourself past the point of being underweight is incredibly unhealthy, both physically and mentally.

Some of the side effects of force your body to extreme weight loss include bone loss and osteoporosis, lowered immune system, fertility problems, and an increased risk of heart disease.

If you want to benefit from the health of the Sirt diet and are underweight, assume the calories, your doctor recommends, along with plenty of sirtfoods.
This will ensure you preserve a healthy weight while also receiving the benefits that sirtuins have to offer.

If you are thin, but still at a BMI of twenty to twenty-five, then you should be safe beginning the Sirt diet, unless otherwise instructed by your doctor.

Can You Eat Meat and Dairy on The Sirtfood Diet?

In many recipes, we choose to use sirtfood sources of protein, such as soy, walnuts, and buckwheat.

This does not mean that you aren't allowed to enjoy meat on the Sirt diet.
It's easy to enjoy a vegetarian or vegan Sirt diet, but if you love your sources of meat, then you don't have to give them up.

Protein is an essential aspect of the Sirt diet to preserve muscle tone, and whether you consume only plant-based proteins or a mixture of plant and animal-based proteins is entirely up to you.

Some meats can help you well utilize the sirtfoods you eat because the amino acid leucine can enhance the effect of sirtfoods. You can find this amino acid in chicken, beef, pork, fish, eggs, dairy, and tofu.

Can I Drink Red Wine during Stage One?

As your calories will be so limited during the first phase, it is not advised to drink alcohol during this phase. Yet, you can enjoy it in moderation during stage two and the maintenance stage.

Chapter 15: Breakfast Recipes Sirtfood

Mushroom Scramble Eggs

Preparation Time: 10 minutes
Cooking Time: 10 minutes
Servings: 4

Ingredients:
- ✓ 2 tbsp
- ✓ 1 teaspoon ground garlic
- ✓ 1 teaspoon mild curry powder
- ✓ 20g lettuce, approximately sliced
- ✓ 1 teaspoon extra virgin olive oil
- ✓ 1/2 bird's eye peeled, thinly chopped
- ✓ a couple of mushrooms, finely chopped
- ✓ 5g parsley, finely chopped

*elective * Insert a seed mix for a topper plus Some Rooster Sauce for taste

Directions:
1. Mix the curry and garlic powder together and then add just a little water until a light glue is obtained.
2. Steam the lettuce for 2 to 3 minutes.
3. Heat the oil over moderate heat in a skillet, and fry the chili and mushrooms for 2 - 3 minutes until they begin to soften and brown.
4. Insert the eggs and spice paste and cook over moderate heat, then add the carrot and then proceed to cook over a moderate heat for a further minute. In the end, put in the parsley, mix well, and function.

Nutrition:
- ✓ Calories: 43 Cal
- ✓ Fat: 2.33 g
- ✓ Protein: 1.25 g
- ✓ Sugar: 0.39 g

Blue Hawaii Smoothie

Preparation Time: 5 minutes
Cooking Time: 0 minutes
Servings: 1

Ingredients:
- 2 tablespoons rings or approximately 4-5 balls
- 1/2 cup frozen tomatoes
- two Tbsp ground flaxseed
- ⅛ cup tender coconut (unsweetened, organic)
- few walnuts
- 1/2 cup fat-free yogurt
- 5-6 ice cubes
- dab of water

Directions:
Throw all of the ingredients together and combine until smooth. You might need to prevent and wake up to receive it combined smoothie or put in more water.

Nutrition:
- Calories: 222 Cal
- Fat: 12.53 g
- Protein: 12.91 g
- Sugar: 11.39 g

Turkey Breakfast Sausages

Preparation Time: 15 minutes
Cooking Time: 20 minutes
Servings: 2

Ingredients:
- 1 lb. extra lean ground turkey
- 1 Tbsp EVOO, and a little more to dirt pan
- 1 Tbsp fennel seeds
- 2 teaspoons smoked paprika
- 1 teaspoon red pepper flakes
- 1 teaspoon peppermint
- 1 teaspoon chicken seasoning
- A couple of shredded cheddar cheese
- A couple of chives, finely chopped
- A few shakes garlic and onion powder
- Two spins of pepper and salt

Directions:
1. Pre Heat oven to 350F.
2. Utilize a little EVOO to dirt a miniature muffin pan.
3. Combine all ingredients and blend thoroughly.
4. Fill each pit on top of the pan and then cook for approximately 15-20 minutes. Each toaster differs; therefore, when muffin fever is 165, then remove.

Nutrition:
- Calories: 168 Cal
- Fat: 44.71 g
- Protein: 285.92 g
- Sugar: 3.71 g

Banana Pecan Muffins

Preparation Time: 20 minutes
Cooking Time: 40 minutes
Servings: 12

Ingredients:
- ✓ 3 Tbsp butter softened
- ✓ 4 ripe bananas
- ✓ 1 Tbsp honey
- ✓ ⅛ cup OJ
- ✓ 1 teaspoon cinnamon
- ✓ 2 cups all-purpose pasta
- ✓ 2 capsules
- ✓ a couple of pecans, sliced
- ✓ 1 Tbsp vanilla

Directions:
1. Preheat the oven to 180ºC.
2. Lightly oil the sides and bottom of the muffin tin and then dust with flour.
3. Dust the surfaces of the tin gently with flour then tap to eradicate any excess.
4. Peel and insert the batter to a mixing bowl and with a fork, mash the carrots; therefore, that you've got a combination of chunky and smooth, then put aside.
5. Insert the orange juice, melted butter, eggs, vanilla, and spices and stir to combine. Roughly chop the pecans onto a chopping board, when using, then fold throughout the mix. Spoon at the batter 3/4 full and bake in the oven for approximately 40 minutes, or until golden and cooked through.

Nutrition:
- ✓ Calories: 132 Cal
- ✓ Fat: 37.04 g
- ✓ Protein: 26.36 g
- ✓ Sugar: 19.65 g

Banana and Blueberry Muffins - SRC

Preparation Time: 20 minutes
Cooking Time: 30 minutes
Servings: 10

Ingredients:

- ✓ 4 large ripe bananas, peeled and mashed
- ✓ 3/4 cup of sugar
- ✓ 1 egg, lightly crushed
- ✓ 1/2 cup of butter, melted (and a little extra to dust the interiors of this muffin tin)
- ✓ 2 cups of blueberries (if they are suspended, do not Defrost them. simply pop them into the batter suspended and)
- ✓ 1 teaspoon baking powder
- ✓ 1 teaspoon baking soda
- ✓ 1/2 teaspoon salt
- ✓ 1 cup of coconut bread
- ✓ 1/2 cup of flour (or 1-1; two cup bread)
- ✓ 1/2 cup applesauce
- ✓ dab of cinnamon

Directions:

1. Add mashed banana to a large mixing bowl.
2. Insert sugar & egg and mix well.
3. Add peanut butter and strawberries.
4. Sift all the dry ingredients together, then add the dry ingredients into the wet mix and mix together lightly.
5. Set into 12 greased muffin cups
6. Bake for 20-30min in 180C or 350 F.

Nutrition:

- ✓ Calories: 203 Cal
- ✓ Fat: 106.48 g
- ✓ Protein: 21.8 g
- ✓ Sugar: 196 g

Morning Meal Sausage Gravy

Preparation Time: 5 minutes
Cooking Time: 5 minutes
Servings: 1

Ingredients:
- ✓ 1 lb. sausage
- ✓ 2 cups 2 percent milk (complete is great also)
- ✓ 1/4 cup entire wheat bread
- ✓ salt and a Lot of pepper to flavor

Directions:
1. Cook sausage from skillet.
2. Add flour and blend cook for about a minute.
3. Insert two cups of milk.
4. Whisk Whilst gravy thickens and bubbles.
5. Add pepper and salt and keep to taste until flawless.
6. Let stand a minute or so to ditch and function over several snacks.

Nutrition:
- ✓ Calories: 260 Cal
- ✓ Fat: 98.99 g
- ✓ Protein: 104.43 g
- ✓ Sugar: 27.05 g

Easy Egg-White Muffins

Preparation Time: 20 minutes
Cooking Time: 1 hour
Servings: 8

Ingredients:
- Language muffin - I enjoy Ezekiel 7 grain
- egg-whites - 6 tbsp or two large egg whites
- turkey bacon or bacon sausage
- sharp cheddar cheese or gouda
- green berry
- discretionary - lettuce, and hot sauce, hummus, flaxseeds, etc.

Directions:
1. At a microwavable safe container, then spray entirely to stop the egg from adhering, then pour egg whites into the dish.
2. Lay turkey bacon or bacon sausage paper towel and then cook.
3. Subsequently, toast your muffin, if preferred.
4. Then put the egg dish in the microwave for 30 minutes. Afterward, with a spoon or fork, then immediately flip egg within the dish and cook for another 30 minutes. Whilst dish remains hot sprinkle some cheese while preparing sausage.
5. The secret is to get a paste of some kind between each coating to put up the sandwich together, i.e., a very small little bit of hummus or even cheese.

Nutrition:
- Calories: 837 Cal
- Fat: 34.95 g
- Protein: 14.71 g
- Sugar: 68.61 g

Sweet Potato Hash

Preparation Time: 10 minutes
Cooking Time: 10 minutes
Servings: 4

Ingredients:

- Inch Sweet-potato
- 1/2 red pepper, diced
- 3 green onions, peppermint
- leftover turkey, then sliced into bits (optional)
- 1 Tbsp of butter - perhaps a bit less (I never quantify)
- carrot powder - a few shakes
- Pepper - only a small dab to get a bit of warmth
- pepper and salt to flavor
- scatter of cheddar cheese (optional)

Directions:

1. Stab a sweet potato and microwave for 5 minutes.
2. Remove from microwave, peel the skin off, and foliage.
3. At a skillet, on medium-high warmth, place peppers and butter and sauté to get a few minutes.
4. Insert potato bits and keep sautéing.
5. Whilst sauté, add sweeteners, leafy vegetables, and green onions.
6. Insert a dab of cheddar and Revel in!

Nutrition:

- Calories: 145 Cal
- Fat: 11.79 g
- Protein: 1.79 g
- Sugar: 5.08 g

Asparagus, Mushroom Artichoke Strata

Preparation Time: 20 minutes
Cooking Time: 15 minutes
Servings: 2

Ingredients:

- ✓ Inch little loaf of sourdough bread
- ✓ 4 challah rolls
- ✓ 8 eggs
- ✓ 2 cups of milk
- ✓ 1 teaspoon salt
- ✓ 1/4 teaspoon black pepper
- ✓ 1 cup Fontina cheese, cut into little chunks
- ✓ 1/2 cup shredded Parmesan cheese
- ✓ 1 Tbsp butter (I used jojoba)
- ✓ 1 teaspoon dried mustard
- ✓ 1/2 can of artichoke hearts, sliced
- ✓ 1 bunch green onions, grated
- ✓ 1 bunch asparagus, cut into 1-inch bits
- ✓ 1 10oz package of baby Bella (cremini) mushrooms, chopped

Directions:

1. Clean mushrooms and slice and trim asparagus and cut in 1-inch pieces. Reserve in a bowl and scatter 1/2 teaspoon salt mixture.
2. Drain and dice 1/2 may or modest artichoke hearts.
3. Melt butter in a pan over moderate heat, also sauté the asparagus and mushrooms before the mushrooms start to brown, about 10 minutes.
4. Blend the artichoke core pieces into a bowl with all a mushroom/asparagus mix. Set aside.
5. Cut or split a tiny sourdough loaf into 1-inch bits. (My loaf was a little too small, therefore that I used 4 challah rolls too)
6. Grease a 9x13 inch baking dish and generate a base coating of bread at the dish. Spread 1/2 cup of Fontina cheese bread, at a coating, and disperse half an apple mixture on the cheese. Lay-down a different layer of these vegetables and bread and high using a 1/2 cup of Fontina cheese.
7. Whisk together eggs, salt, milk, dry mustard, and pepper into a bowl and then pour the egg mixture on the vegetables and bread.
8. Cover the dish, and then simmer for 3 weeks.
9. Pre Heat oven to 375 degrees.
10. Eliminate the casserole from the fridge and let stand for half an hour.
11. Spread All the Parmesan cheese at a coating within the strata.
12. Bake in the preheated oven until a time when a knife inserted near the border comes out clean, 40 to 45 minutes. Allow it stand 5 to 10 minutes before cutting into squares.

Nutrition: (Calories: 350 Cal | Fat: 169 g | Protein: 181 g | Sugar: 49.76 g)

Egg White Veggie Wontons W/Fontina Topped W/ Crispy Prosciutto

Preparation Time: 15 minutes
Cooking Time: 15 minutes
Servings: 4

Ingredients:

- 1 cup egg whites
- butter
- fontina cheese
- mixed shredded cheddar cheese
- broccoli I utilized wheat, chopped bits
- tomatoes - diced
- salt and pepper
- prosciutto - two pieces
- Remove Won Ton wrappers out of the freezer.

Directions:

1. Pre Heat oven to 350.
2. Spray miniature cupcake tin with cooking spray.
3. After wrappers begin to defrost, peel off them carefully - apart, one at a time and press cupcake tin lightly.
4. I sliced the wrappers having a little bit of peanut butter. (optional)
5. set a chunk of cheese in every bottom.
6. Satisfy desired lettuce - I used pre-cooked broccoli bits and diced tomatoes.
7. Pour egg whites all toppings.
8. Sprinkle each with some of those shredded cheddar cheese.
9. Cook for approximately 15 minutes, but get started watching them afterward 10 - whenever they poof up - assess them poking the middle with a fork.
10. While eggs are cooking, then spray a sheet of foil with cooking spray and then put 2 pieces of prosciutto onto it and then cook at exactly the exact same period as the egg whites. After 8 minutes, then take and let sit once it cools it becomes crispy and chop and high eggs!

Nutrition:

- Calories: 298 Cal
- Fat: 11 g
- Protein: 24 g
- Sugar: 6 g

Chapter 16: Power Juice and Cocktail Recipes

Lemonade Redneck

Preparation Time: 5 minutes
Cooking Time: 5 minutes
Servings: 1

Ingredients:
- ✓ Bourbon
- ✓ Ice cubes
- ✓ Lemonade
- ✓ A slice of lemon

Directions:
1. Take your mason jar
2. Fill it with ice cubes
3. Pour bourbon
4. Add the lemonade
5. Slice a lemon
6. Add the slices to the pot
7. Serve (without straw, it's more authentic but it's less practical)

Nutrition:
- ✓ Calories: 11 Cal
- ✓ Fat: 0.12 g
- ✓ Protein: 0.17 g
- ✓ Sugar: 1.21 g

Coffee Latte Milkshake

Preparation Time: 2 minutes
Cooking Time: 2 minutes
Servings: 1

Ingredients:
- 350ml cold coffee (1 1/2 cups)
- 2 scoops of vanilla ice cream
- 2 tablespoons chocolate syrup or even better, Hot fudge
- Whipped cream
- Squares of "rich" dark chocolate - dessert type

Directions:
1. Take a blender
2. Pour coffee
3. Put the scoops of ice cream
4. Pour syrup
5. Mix well
6. Optional: pour some chocolate syrup coulis into the glass, tilting it diagonally, as if you were
7. pouring beer. It's super beautiful but be careful, you have to pour the milkshake gently after
8. Pour the milkshake into the glass
9. Cover with whipped cream
10. Chop the chocolate over the top and serve

Nutrition:
- Calories: 218 Cal
- Fat: 0.88 g
- Protein: 1.64 g
- Sugar: 38.73 g

Berry and Beet Smoothie

Preparation Time: 5 minutes
Cooking Time: 5 minutes
Servings: 1

Ingredients:
- 1 cup of pineapple juice
- 1 cup of low-fat or fat-free vanilla yogurt
- 1 cup of fresh or frozen strawberries
- ½ cup of fresh or frozen blueberries
- ½ cup of beet canned sliced, drained

Directions:
1. Combine all ingredients in a blender.
2. Mix until smooth.
3. Serve immediately.
4. Refrigerate or freeze what is leftover during the following 2 hours.

Notes : For a thicker smoothie, use frozen fruit instead of fresh fruit.
5. Use plain yogurt and ½ teaspoon of vanilla.
6. Add a banana.

Nutrition:
- Calories: 662 Cal
- Fat: 4.68 g
- Protein: 16.54 g
- Sugar: 123.81 g

Green Pineapple Smoothie

Preparation Time: 5 minutes
Cooking Time: 5 minutes
Servings: 1

Ingredients:
- ✓ 50 grams of chard
- ✓ 1 apple
- ✓ 200 grams of pineapple
- ✓ 1 tsp. of flax seeds

Directions:
All to the glass of the blender with a little water and grind well.

Nutrition:
- ✓ Calories: 251 Cal
- ✓ Fat: 4.11 g
- ✓ Protein: 7.3 g
- ✓ Sugar: 48.36 g

Blue Hawaii

The first Blue Hawaii was made by Harry Yee, the chief bartender at the Hilton Hawaiian Village Hotel in Waikiki. Yee had to create a blue cocktail when a representative from a well-known distillery demanded a drink with that hue, since he was promoting Curaçao. Although the combination of ingredients has evolved, Blue Hawaii maintains rum as a base drink and the classic umbrella as the garnish.

Preparation Time: 5 minutes
Cooking Time: 5 minutes
Servings: 1

Ingredients:
- 60 ml of rum
- 30 ml of blue Curaçao
- 30 ml of orange juice
- 60 ml of pineapple juice

Directions:
Mix all ingredients inside a cocktail shaker with ice and shake well for a few seconds. Garnish the glass using a slice of pineapple or orange and serve. It has no loss, but if you are one of those who prefers to trace the movements of an expert, here is an example. Remember, Blue Hawaii is ideal to consume before eating, on a terrace in the sun.

Nutrition:
- Calories: 413 Cal
- Fat: 10.75 g
- Protein: 57.12 g
- Sugar: 0 g

Daiquiri

Thinking of Daiquiri is thinking of the beach, palm trees, music, summer ... is thinking of Cuba. There is born this cocktail that is ordered in bars around the world and whose basic alcohol is white rum. The daiquiri owes its name to a beach near Santiago de Cuba and its origin to an American named Jennings Cox, who had to improvise a drink for his guests when he ran out of Geneva. And he mixed three

Preparation Time: 5 minutes
Cooking Time: 5 minutes
Servings: 1

Ingredients:

- ✓ 42 ml of white rum
- ✓ Juice of half a lemon (about 7 ml)
- ✓ 1 tablespoon of sugar

Directions:

The daiquiri was one of Ernest Hemingway's favorite drinks, that whenever he traveled to Cuba, he passed by La Floridita, a bar that claims to be the birthplace of the daiquiri and that hundreds of celebrities have visited since the American writer recommended it. So, if you want to have one of the best daiquiris in the world, stop by Havana. Although the original cocktail was made with lemon, it is easy to find strawberry, banana or assorted fruit daiquiris. Other variations lead us to the Floridita Daiquiri, which contains maraschino liqueur, or the Papa-Papa, in which the quantities are doubled and grapefruit is added.

Nutrition:

- ✓ Calories: 36 Cal
- ✓ Fat: 0.06 g
- ✓ Protein: 0.08 g
- ✓ Sugar: 8.43 g

Spinach Smoothie

Preparation Time: 5 minutes
Cooking Time: 5 minutes
Servings: 1

Ingredients:
- 1 large hand spinach (50 grams)
- 1 pear
- ½ banana
- ¼ zucchini
- 100 ml unsweetened almond milk
- 100 ml of water

Directions:
Get a blender; pour all the ingredients inside it, and then blend.

Nutrition:
- Calories: 1 Cal
- Fat: 0.01 g
- Protein: 0.08 g
- Sugar: 0 g

Kale Smoothie

Preparation Time: 5 minutes
Cooking Time: 5 minutes
Servings: 1

Ingredients:
- 1 large hand kale (50 grams)
- ½ mango
- ½ banana
- 1 tbsp chia seed
- 100 ml unsweetened coconut milk
- 150 ml of water

Directions:
Get a blender; pour all the ingredients into it, and then blend.

Nutrition:
- Calories: 290 Cal
- Fat: 15 g
- Protein: 68 g
- Sugar: 100 g

Avocado Smoothie

Preparation Time: 5 minutes
Cooking Time: 5 minutes
Servings: 1

Ingredients:
- ½ avocado
- 1 banana
- Hand of spinach
- 1 tbsp. linseed
- 100 ml unsweetened almond milk
- 100 ml of water

Directions:
Get a blender; pour all the ingredients into it, and then blend.

Nutrition:
- Calories: 161 Cal
- Fat: 14.73 g
- Protein: 2.01 g
- Sugar: 0.66 g

Lettuce Smoothie

Preparation Time: 5 minutes
Cooking Time: 5 minutes
Servings: 1

Ingredients:
- 2 hands turn
- 3 fresh plums, seeded
- ½ banana
- 1 tbsp. linseed
- ½ cucumbers
- 200 ml unsweetened almond milk

Directions:
Get a blender; pour all the ingredients into it, and then blend.

Nutrition:
- Calories: 135 Cal
- Fat: 0.3 g
- Protein: 1.09 g
- Sugar: 32.17 g

Chapter 17: Main Meal Recipes

Baked Potatoes with Spicy Chickpea Stew Fillet Diablo

Preparation Time: 10 minutes
Cooking Time: 15 minutes
Servings: 2

Ingredients:
- 2 fillets of sole (5 ounces each)
- 1 teaspoon lemon juice
- 1/2 teaspoon salt
- Garnish
- 2 thin lemon slices, chopped fresh parsley, and parsley sprigs
- 2 teaspoons margarine
- 1 teaspoon all-purpose flour
- 1/4 cup water
- 2 tablespoons dry white wine
- 1 teaspoon Dijon-style mustard
- 1 teaspoon drained capers
- 1/2 teaspoon grated lemon rind
- 1/2 teaspoon white pepper, divided

Directions:
In small saucepan heat margarine until bubbly and hot. Sprinkle with flour and stir quickly to combine; cook over low heat, constantly stirring, for 1 minute. Remove from heat; stir in water, wine, and mustard. Return to heat and bring mixture to a boil; reduce heat and let simmer, constantly stirring, until sauce is thickened. Stir in capers, lemon rind, and dash pepper; remove from heat and keep warm.

Sprinkle sole fillets with lemon juice and remaining pepper. Spray rack of broiling pan with nonstick cooking spray; transfer fish to rack and broil until fish flakes easily when tested with a fork, about 5 minutes. Sprinkle fillets with salt, then transfer to a serving platter. Spoon sauce over fish; garnish with lemon and parsley.

Nutrition:
- Calories: 167 Cal
- Fat: 5 g
- Protein: 24 g
- Sugar: 4.14 g

Artichoke-Stuffed Red Snapper

Preparation Time: 40 minutes
Cooking Time: 50 minutes
Servings: 6

Ingredients:

- 1 tablespoon vegetable oil
- 3/4 cup finely chopped onions
- 1/2 cups frozen artichoke hearts, thawed and chopped
- 3 slices white bread, toasted and made into fine crumbs
- 1/4 cup each chopped fresh parsley and lemon juice
- 1 teaspoon salt
- 1/2 teaspoon pepper
- 1 red snapper,
- 3 pounds dressed with head and tail left on 1 cup mixed vegetable juice

Directions:

Preheat oven to 350°F. In 9-inch skillet heat oil; add onions and sauté until translucent. Add artichoke hearts and sauté for 3 minutes longer. Stir in bread crumbs, parsley, lemon juice, salt, and pepper; remove from heat and allow the mixture to cool slightly.

Stuff fish with artichoke mixture, using toothpicks or wooden skewers to close the cavity. Spray baking dish that is large enough to hold fish flat with nonstick cooking spray; transfer stuffed snapper to a dish and pour vegetable juice over fish. Bake, frequently basting with pan juices, until fish flakes easily at the touch of a fork, 40 to 50 minutes.

Nutrition:

- Calories: 218 Cal
- Fat: 13 g
- Protein: 31 g
- Sugar: 11.25 g

Sesame Chicken Salad

Preparation Time: 10 minutes
Cooking Time: 12 minutes
Servings: 2

Ingredients:
- 1 tbsp sesame seeds
- One cucumber, peeled, half-long, desired with a teaspoon and 100 g sliced baby kale, roughly chopped
- 60 g Pak choi, very finely shredded
- 1/2 red onion, very finely sliced
- A big handful (20 g) of petroleum, chopped
- 150 g cooked chicken, shredded
- For dressing:
- 1 tbsp of extra virgin olive oil
- 1 tsp of sesame oil
- One lime juice
- 1 tsp of sugar
- 2 tsp of soy sauce

Directions:
1. In A hot frying pan, the sesame seeds toast for 2 minutes until lightly browned and fragrant.
2. Move to a cold plate.
3. Combine the olive oil, sesame oil, lime juice, honey, and soy sauce in a small bowl to make a dressing.
4. In a large bowl, put the cucumber, the kale, the Pak choi, the red onion, and the parsley and combine gently. Pour over the sauce, then again blend.
5. Divide the salad with the shredded chicken between two plates, and top. Just before eating, brush over the sesame seeds.

Nutrition:
- Calories: 304 Cal
- Fat: 95.86 g
- Protein: 74.38 g
- Sugar: 6.37 g

Sirt Food Miso-Marinated Cod with Stir-Fried Greens

Preparation Time: 10 minutes
Cooking Time: 10 minutes
Servings: 2

Ingredients:

- 20g miso
- 1 tbsp mirin
- 1 tbsp of extra virgin olive oil
- 200 g of skinless cod fillet
- 20 g of red onion, sliced
- 40 g of celery, sliced
- One garlic clove, finely chopped
- One bird's eye chili, finely chopped
- 1 tsp of fresh ginger
- 60 g of green beans
- 50 g of kale, roughly chopped
- 1 tsp of sesame seeds
- 5 g of parsley, roughly chopped
- 1 tbsp of tamari
- 30 g of buckwheat
- 1 tsp of turmeric

Directions:

Mix the miso, mirin, and oil in a tablespoon. Rub the cod all over and leave for 30 minutes to marinate. Bake the cod for about 10 minutes.

Meanwhile, heat the remaining oil to a large frying pan or wok. Stir-fry the onion for a few minutes, then add the celery, garlic, chili, ginger, green beans, and kale. Toss and fry until the kale is cooked through and tender. To aid the cooking process, you might need to add a little water to the pan. Cook the buckwheat with the turmeric for 3 minutes according to the directions on the packet. To the stir-fry, add the sesame seeds, parsley, and tamari and serve with the greens and fish.

Nutrition:

- Calories: 355 Cal
- Fat: 10.87 g
- Protein: 40.31 g
- Sugar: 5.17 g

Raspberry and Blackcurrant Jelly-Sirtfood Recipes

Preparation Time: 15 minutes
Cooking Time: 15 minutes plus setting time
Servings: 3

Ingredients:

- ✓ 100g raspberries washed
- ✓ Two leaves
- ✓ 100g blackcurrants washed and stalked removed
- ✓ 2 tbsp granulated sugar
- ✓ 300ml water

Directions:

1. Two of your SIRT 5 a day, making a jelly ahead of time, is a perfect way to prepare the fruit, so it's ready to eat the first morning.
2. Put the raspberries in two plates/glasses/molds. Place the gelatin leaves softening in a bowl of cold water.
3. Put the blackcurrants with the sugar and 100ml water in a small saucepan and bring to a boil.
4. Simmer hard for 5 minutes, then remove from heat. Put on for 2 minutes.
5. Squeeze the gelatin leaves out of the excess water and add to the saucepan. Remove until completely dissolved, and then mix in the remaining water. The jellies should be ready overnight or in around 3-4 hours.

Nutrition:

- ✓ Calories: 142 Cal
- ✓ Fat: 1 g
- ✓ Protein: 4.18 g
- ✓ Sugar: 20.07 g

Strawberry Buckwheat Tabouleh

Preparation Time: 15 minutes
Cooking Time: 15 minutes
Servings: 4

Ingredients:
- 50 g of buckwheat
- 1 tbsp of turmeric
- 80 g of avocado
- 65 g of tomato
- 20 g of red onion
- 25 g of Medjool dates, pitted
- 1 tbsp seed, 30 g of parsley
- 100 g of strawberries, hulled
- 1 tbsp of extra virgin olive oil
- 1/2 lemon juice, 30 g of rocket

Directions:
Cook the buckwheat with the turmeric, as indicated on the packet. Drain to cool and hold to one side. Cut the avocado, tomato, red onion, eggs, capers, and peregrinate thinly and blend with the cold buckwheat. Slice the strawberries, then mix the oil and lemon juice gently into the salad. Serve on a bed of rocket.

Nutrition:
- Calories: 382 Cal
- Fat: 19.34 g
- Protein: 6.5 g
- Sugar: 23.84 g

Buckwheat and Nut Loaf

Preparation Time: 15 minutes
Cooking Time: 15 minutes
Servings: 4

Ingredients:
- 225g/8 oz. buckwheat
- 2 tbsp olive oil
- 225g/8 of mushrooms
- 2-3 carrots, finely diced
- 2-3 tbsp of fresh herbs, finely chopped
- 225g/8 of nuts, e.g., hazelnuts, almonds, walnuts
- Two eggs, beaten (or 2 tbsp tahini for vegan version), salt and pepper

Directions:
Place the buckwheat in a 350 ml/1,5 cup pan with water and a pinch of salt. Take to simmer. Cover and cook with the lid until all the water is absorbed about 10-15 minutes. Blitz, the food processor's nuts, until well chopped.

Stir in the eggs and mix the potatoes, cooked buckwheat, herbs, and chopped nuts. If you use tahini instead of eggs, combine this with some water before combining it in the buckwheat to create a thick consistency of pouring. Switch to a lined or oiled loaf tin and bake for 30 minutes in the oven at gas mark 5/190C until set and just brown on top.

Nutrition:
- Calories: 279 Cal
- Fat: 19.1 g
- Protein: 69.8 g
- Sugar: 19.69 g

Moong Dahl

Preparation Time: 10 minutes
Cooking Time: 15 minutes
Servings: 5

Ingredients:

- 300g/10 of split mung beans (Moong Dahl)–preferably soaked for a few hours
- 600ml/1pt water
- Two tbsp/30 g olive oil, butter or ghee
- One red onion, finely chopped
- 1-2 tsp of coriander seeds
- 1-2 tsp of cumin seeds
- 2-4 tsp of fresh ginger, chopped
- 1-2 tsp of turmeric
- ¼ tsp of cayenne pepper–more if you want it spicy
- Salt & black pepper to taste

Directions:

1. Drain and rinse split mung beans. Place in a casserole, and cover with water. Bring to the boil and skim off any moisture that comes up. Turn the heat down, cover and simmer.
2. In a heavy-bottomed pan, dry fry the coriander and cumin seeds until they begin to pop. Grind them in a mortar and pestle.
3. Attach the ground spices and the ginger, turmeric, and cayenne pepper to the onions. Cook in a couple of minutes.

Nutrition:

- Calories: 430 Cal
- Fat: 32.1 g
- Protein: 12.37 g
- Sugar: 17.3 g

Polenta Bake

Preparation Time: 20 minutes
Cooking Time: 50 minutes
Servings: 10

Ingredients:

- ✓ 850ml/1.5 pints of water
- ✓ 1 tsp of rock salt or sea salt
- ✓ 200g/7 of coarse yellow polenta
- ✓ 2 tsp of dried oregano
- ✓ 1 cup of sun-dried tomatoes
- ✓ Chopped, three eggs, separated
- ✓ 1-2 tbsp of butter or olive oil
- ✓ Freshly ground black pepper
- ✓ 300g/10 of cheddar or red Leicester cheese rubbed (optional)

Directions:

1. To cook the polenta, bring the water to a boil in a large salt pan.
2. Slowly pour in the boiling polenta the whole time. Remove the sun-dried tomatoes and the oregano.
3. Cook on low heat, as long as the polenta packet instructions suggest. It could be from 3 minutes to 40 minutes at any location. Remove to prevent clumping and to stick on frequently. Whereas the polenta cooks whip the egg whites until they form steep peaks.
4. When cooking the polenta, turn off the heat and mix egg yolks and black pepper in 1-2 tbsp of butter or olive oil together with 2/3 of the cheese, if used. Carefully insert the egg whites into the polenta mix.
5. Move the mixture to an evidence dish oiled with an oven: spread and the top smooth.
6. Sprinkle over the remaining grated cheese.
7. Bake for 40-50 minutes at gas mark 4/180C/350F, until set and start to brown.

Nutrition:

- ✓ Calories: 234 Cal
- ✓ Fat: 135.39 g
- ✓ Protein: 102.98 g
- ✓ Sugar: 25.37 g

Cajun Steak and Veg Rice Jar Recipe

Preparation Time: 15 minutes
Cooking Time: 20 minutes
Servings: 1

Ingredients:
- 1 tablespoon vegetable oil
- 1 celery stick, finely chopped
- 3 large carrots, sliced into rounds
- 250g frozen chopped mixed peppers
- 4 spring onions, chopped, green and white parts split
- 500g 5 percent beef mince
- 2 teaspoon seasoning
- 1 teaspoon tomato purée
- 2 x 250g packs ready-cooked long-grain rice

Directions:
1. Heat the oil in a large, shallow skillet over moderate heat. Add the carrots, celery, peppers, and snowy areas of the nuts. Cook for 10 mins before the veg is beginning to soften.
2. Insert the mince, season liberally, and cook for 10 mins before mince is browned and start to really go crispy.
3. Insert the Cajun seasoning and tomato purée; stir fry to coat the mince. Hint inside the rice combined with 4 tablespoons of plain water. Stir to completely unite heat and heat until the rice is hot. Scatter on the rest of the spring onion before serving.

Nutrition:
- Calories: 398 Cal
- Fat: 96.64 g
- Protein: 135.12 g
- Sugar: 16.8 g

Chapter Eighteen: Stir Fry Recipes

Chicken and Green Beans

Preparation Time: 6 minutes
Cooking Time: 10 minutes
Servings: 4

Ingredients:
- Toasted peanuts, for sprinkling
- For the Marinade:
- 1½ teaspoons cornstarch
- ½ teaspoon red pepper flakes, or to taste
- Salt, to taste
- 1 tablespoon soy sauce

For the Sauce:
- 2 tablespoons soy sauce, divided
- 2 tablespoons seasoned rice vinegar
- 2 tablespoons Chinese cooking wine
- 1-pound chicken thighs or breasts, boneless, skinless, sliced thinly against the grain
- 2 tablespoons of vegetable oil, broken down
- 6 Scallions, trimmed ends, cut into 1 "pieces
- 1 (2-inch) piece of ginger, sliced
- ¾ pound green beans, trimmed and halved
- Salt, to taste

Directions:
1. Combine marinade ingredients in a bowl, add chicken slices and toss.
2. In a small bowl, stir sauce ingredients together. Set aside.
3. In a wok, skillet, or frying pan, heat 1 tablespoon oil to shimmering.
4. Add Ginger and Scallion. Stir-fry until brown (roughly 2 minutes).
5. Add green beans and a pinch of salt, tossing until crisp-tender (about 4 minutes). Transfer
6. veggies to a platter and keep the wok warm.
7. Add remaining oil and adjust heat to high.
8. When the oil is almost smoking, lay the chicken on the wok and let cook until underside is
9. browned (about 1 minute).
10. Stir-fry for 1–2 minutes, or until evenly browned.
11. Stir in sauce and veggies.
12. Toss until sauce is thickened (about 30 seconds).
13. Remove from heat and season with more salt, if needed.
14. Sprinkle with toasted nuts and serve with rice.

Nutrition: *(Calories: 563 Cal | Fat: 35 g | Protein: 84 g | Sugar: 13 g)*

Moo Goo Gai Pan (Mushrooms with Chicken)

Preparation Time: 5 minutes (add 15 minutes marinating time)
Cooking Time: 10 minutes
Servings: 2 - 4

Ingredients:
- ¾ pound chicken breasts, boneless and skinless, sliced thinly
- 3 tablespoons vegetable oil, divided
- 1 cup fresh button mushrooms, sliced
- ½ cup canned bamboo shoots, rinsed and drained
- ½ cup canned water chestnuts, rinsed and drained
- 1 thumb ginger, chopped
- 1 clove garlic, minced

For the Marinade:
- 2 tablespoons soy sauce
- 1 tablespoon Chinese cooking wine
- ½ teaspoon sesame oil, or to taste
- 1 tablespoon cornstarch

For the Sauce:
- ½ cup chicken stock or broth
- 2 tablespoons oyster sauce
- 1 teaspoon sugar
- 1 tablespoon cornstarch

Directions:
1. Combine ingredients for the marinade in a bowl with chicken. Rub into chicken and let marinate for 15 minutes.
2. In a bowl, mix sauce ingredients together and set aside.
3. In a wok, skillet, or frying pan, heat 2 tablespoons of oil.
4. Add the chicken to the surface and stir-fry until browned (about 3–5 minutes). Transfer onto a platform.
5. Add remaining oil to wok and stir-fry ginger and garlic until fragrant (about 30 seconds).
6. Stir in mushrooms and stir-fry for about 1 minute.
7. Add bamboo shoots and water chestnuts, stir-frying to heat through.
8. Give reserved sauce mixture a quick stir and pour into wok.
9. Cook, with stirring, until thickened.
10. Return chicken to wok and stir until well-coated and cooked through.

Nutrition: *(Calories: 416 Cal | Fat: 15 g | Protein: 24 g | Sugar: 11.65 g)*

Garlic Chicken

Preparation Time: 5 minutes
Cooking Time: 15 minutes
Servings: 4

Ingredients:
- 1 1/2 Tablespoons of vegetable oil, broken down
- 1 pound of skinless, bare chicken breast cut into pieces of bite-size
- Salt and pepper to taste
- 1 cup broccoli florets
- 1 cup mushrooms, halved
- 1 yellow bell pepper, sliced thinly
- 4 cloves garlic, minced
- For the Sauce:
- ¾ cup chicken broth
- 1½ teaspoons sugar
- 1 tablespoon soy sauce
- 2 teaspoons sesame oil
- 2 teaspoons cornstarch

Directions:
1. In a bowl, stir ingredients of the sauce together and set aside.
2. Heat 1 spoonful of oil over high heat in a wok, skillet, or frying pan.
3. Add chicken, and add salt and pepper to season.
4. Stir-fry until browned on the surface (about 7 minutes). Transfer to a plate.
5. Add remaining oil to wok and heat over medium-high heat.
6. Add the broccoli, mushrooms, and bell pepper and stir-fry until tender (about 5 minutes).
7. Reduce heat to medium.
8. Add the garlic and stir-fry (about 30 seconds) until fragrant.
9. Back to wok chicken.
10. Give a quick stir to prepared sauce mixture and pour it into a wok.
11. Bring sauce to a boil and let simmer until thickened (about 2 minutes). Adjust flavor with more
12. salt and pepper, if needed.
13. Serve hot.

Nutrition: (Calories: 215 Cal | Fat: 6.3 g | Protein: 24 g | Sugar: 11.26 g)

Cashew Chicken

Preparation Time: 5 minutes plus 20 minutes marinating time
Cooking Time: 10 minutes
Servings: 3 - 4

Ingredients:
- ✓ 1-pound boneless, skinless chicken breasts, cubed
- ✓ 3–4 tablespoons oil for stir-frying, divided
- ✓ 1 clove garlic, minced
- ✓ 1 tablespoon green onion, chopped
- ✓ ¼ cup roasted cashew nuts

For the Marinade:
- ✓ 1 tablespoon Chinese cooking wine
- ✓ 2 teaspoons freshly squeezed ginger juice
- ✓ ½ teaspoon salt
- ✓ 1 tablespoon cornstarch

For the Sauce:
- ✓ 2 tablespoons hoisin sauce
- ✓ 2 tablespoons dark soy sauce
- ✓ 2 tablespoons water
- ✓ 1 teaspoon granulated sugar

Directions:
1. Combine the first 3 marinade ingredients and add chicken. Sprinkle with cornstarch and rub to coat. Let marinate for 20 minutes.
2. Stir sauce ingredients together in a bowl and set aside.
3. Heat 2 tablespoons oil in a wok, skillet, or frying pan over medium-high heat.
4. Add garlic and stir-fry until fragrant (about 30 seconds).
5. Add chicken and stir-fry until browned on the outside (about 5–7 minutes). Transfer to a plate.
6. Add remaining oil (about 1–2 tablespoons, or as needed) to wok.
7. Add green onion and stir-fry until tender.
8. Return chicken to wok and stir just to heat through.
9. Add sauce ingredients and cook until thickened.
10. Add cashews and stir until ingredients are well-coated with sauce.
11. Serve hot.

Nutrition: Calories: 396 Cal | Fat: 19 g | Protein: 34 g | Sugar: 43.62 g

Creamy Curry Chicken with Vegetables

Preparation Time: 25 minutes
Cooking Time: 15 minutes
Servings: 4

Ingredients:
- ✓ 1-pound boneless chicken breasts, cubed into small pieces
- ✓ 4 tablespoons green curry paste
- ✓ 1 cup reduced-fat coconut milk
- ✓ ½ cup chicken stock
- ✓ 2 zucchinis, sliced thinly
- ✓ 1 onion, diced
- ✓ 2 Asian eggplant (long and thin), sliced thinly
- ✓ 1 cup of broccoli, chopped into florets
- ✓ 2 tablespoons fresh basil
- ✓ ¼ teaspoon cayenne pepper, more if you like it spicier
- ✓ 1 teaspoon curry powder
- ✓ 2 tablespoons grapeseed oil
- ✓ 2 cups cooked brown or white rice for serving (optional)

Directions:
1. Heat oil on medium-high heat. When hot, add onion and curry paste and cook for 2 minutes.
2. Add chicken and stir-fry for 4-5 minutes. Be sure to coat it in the curry paste.
3. Add coconut milk and stock and bring to a boil. Turn down the heat to medium-low and let simmer for a few minutes.
4. Add the rest of the vegetables and the spices and cook until chicken is tender.
5. Serve over rice, if desired.

Nutrition:
- ✓ Calories: 300 Cal
- ✓ Fat: 11 g
- ✓ Protein: 28 g
- ✓ Sugar: 56.36 g

Simple Beef Stir-fry

Preparation Time: 15 minutes
Cooking Time: 25 minutes
Servings: 4

Ingredients:

- ✓ 2 cups vegetable stock
- ✓ 2 tablespoons soy sauce
- ✓ 4 garlic cloves, chopped
- ✓ 2 teaspoons chili powder
- ✓ 1-pound top sirloin beef, thinly sliced
- ✓ 3 cups broccoli, chopped into florets
- ✓ 1 cup cremini mushrooms, sliced
- ✓ 1 cup sugar snaps peas
- ✓ 4 green onions, sliced
- ✓ 1 tablespoon fresh ginger, peeled and sliced
- ✓ 2 tablespoons grapeseed oil

Directions:

1. Prepare the marinade in a shallow dish or a re-sealable plastic bag such as a Ziplock bag, Mix vegetable stock, soy sauce, and chili powder. If you desire more spices, add ½ teaspoon cayenne pepper. Toss the beef in the sauce and marinate for 10-15 minutes.
2. On high heat, add oil to the wok and when hot, put in ginger, broccoli, mushrooms, peas, green onions, and ¼ of the marinade, cook for about 3 minutes or until the broccoli softens. Add beef and remaining marinade and cook until beef is browned. Serve hot.

Nutrition:

- ✓ Calories: 390 Cal
- ✓ Fat: 21 g
- ✓ Protein: 30 g
- ✓ Sugar: 26 g

Easy Shiitake Stir-fry

Preparation Time: 2 minutes
Cooking Time: 7 – 10 minutes
Servings: 2

Ingredients:
- 2 tablespoons peanut oil
- 1 (½-inch) piece ginger, peeled and minced
- 1 clove garlic, minced
- ½ pound fresh shiitake mushrooms, sliced
- 1–2 tablespoons soy sauce
- 1 tablespoon sesame oil
- 1 green onion, chopped
- 2 teaspoons toasted sesame seeds

Directions:
1. Heat peanut oil in a wok, skillet, or frying pan over medium-high heat.
2. Stir-fry ginger and garlic until fragrant (about 30 seconds).
3. Add sliced shiitake and stir-fry until soft and lightly browned (about 2–3 minutes).
4. Stir in soy sauce and sesame oil.
5. Continue to stir-fry until most liquid has evaporated.
6. Sprinkle with green onion and sesame seeds.
7. Serve.

Nutrition:
- Calories: 283 Cal
- Fat: 22.9 g
- Protein: 3.8 g
- Sugar: 19.7 g

Okra Stir-fry

Preparation Time: 5 minutes
Cooking Time: 5 minutes
Servings: 2

Ingredients:

- 1 tablespoon peanut or vegetable oil
- 1 teaspoon Sichuan peppercorn
- 2 dried chili peppers, chopped
- 7 ounces okra, cut into bite-size pieces
- 2 teaspoons light soy sauce

Directions:

1. Heat oil in a wok, skillet, or frying pan over medium heat. Stir-fry Sichuan peppercorn until dark and fragrant (about 1 minute). Fish out the peppercorns and discard.
2. Add chili and stir-fry briefly (about 30 seconds).
3. Adjust heat to high.
4. Add okra and stir-fry to blanch and coat with oil (1 minute).
5. Add soy sauce. Reduce heat, if needed.
6. Continue stir-frying until okra is cooked through (about 3 minutes).
7. Serve hot.

Nutrition:

- Calories: 100 Cal
- Fat: 7 g
- Protein: 2.4 g
- Sugar: 8.9 g

Simple Stir-Fried Bok Choy

Preparation Time: 5 minutes
Cooking Time: 10 minutes
Servings: 4

Ingredients:
- 1½ pounds bok choy, trimmed and washed
- 2 tablespoons cooking oil
- 2 cloves garlic, finely minced
- 1 teaspoon grated ginger
- 3 tablespoons water, broth or cooking wine
- 1 teaspoon soy sauce
- ½ teaspoon sesame oil

Directions:
1. Add oil to wok, skillet, or frying pan.
2. Add garlic and ginger before the oil has been heated (this is to avoid burning the aromatics and
3. to infuse more flavor into the oil).
4. Set heat at medium-high.
5. Stir-fry when sizzling starts.
6. When fragrant and oil is adequately hot, stir in bok choy. Stir-fry to coat well with flavored oil and to cook evenly, until leaves turn bright green (about 15–30 seconds).
7. Splash with water, cover, and let steam for 1 minute.
8. Stir in soy sauce.
9. Remove from heat.
10. Drizzle with sesame oil and serve hot.

Nutrition:
- Calories: 91 Cal
- Fat: 11 g
- Protein: 2 g
- Sugar: 4 g

Lettuce Stir-fry

Preparation Time: 2 minutes
Cooking Time: 5 minutes
Servings: 4 - 6

Ingredients:

- 1½ teaspoons soy sauce
- 1½ teaspoons sesame oil
- 1 teaspoon of rice wine
- ¾ teaspoon sugar
- 1 tablespoon peanut or canola oil
- 3 cloves garlic, peeled and minced
- 1 head iceberg lettuce, rinsed, dried, and torn into large pieces
- Salt and pepper, to taste

Directions:

1. In a small bowl, stir together soy sauce, sesame oil, rice wine, and sugar. Set aside.
2. Heat oil in a wok, skillet, or frying pan over medium-high heat.
3. Stir-fry garlic until lightly browned.
4. Add lettuce and stir-fry very briefly until bright in color but still crisp.
5. Stir in sauce and season with salt and pepper.
6. Serve immediately.

Nutrition:

- Calories: 72 Cal
- Fat: 5.3 g
- Protein: 1.6 g
- Sugar: 5.7 g

Chapter 19: Sweets

Dark Chocolate Mousse (Vegan)

Preparation Time: 10 minutes
Cooking Time: 2 hours plus cooling time
Servings: 4

Ingredients:
- ✓ 1 (16 ounce) package silken tofu, drained
- ✓ ½ cup pure maple syrup
- ✓ 1 teaspoon pure vanilla extract
- ✓ ¼ cup soymilk
- ✓ ½ cup unsweetened cocoa powder
- ✓ Mint leaves (optional and highly encouraged)

Directions:
1. Place tofu, maple syrup and vanilla in a food processor or blender. Process until well blended.
2. Add remaining ingredients and process until mixture is fully blended.
3. Pour into small dessert cups or espresso cups. Chill for at least 2 hours.

Nutrition:
- ✓ Calories: 544 Cal
- ✓ Fat: 6.95 g
- ✓ Protein: 8.82 g
- ✓ Sugar: 99.75 g

Loaded Chocolate Fudge

Preparation Time: 10 minutes
Cooking Time: 1 hour plus cooling time
Servings: 16

Ingredients:

- ✓ 1 cup Medjool dates, chopped
- ✓ 2 tablespoons coconut oil, melted
- ✓ 1/2 cup peanut butter
- ✓ ¼ cup of unsweetened cocoa powder
- ✓ ½ cup walnuts
- ✓ 1 teaspoon vanilla

Directions:

1. Soak the dates in warm water for 20 – 30 minutes Lightly grease an 8" square baking pan with coconut oil.
2. Add dates, peanut butter, cocoa powder and vanilla to a food processer and blend until smooth.
3. Fold in walnuts.
4. Pack into the greased baking pan and put in your freezer for 1 hour or until fudge is solid and firm.
5. Cut into 16 or more bite-sized squares and store in a semi-airtight container in the refrigerator.

Nutrition:

- ✓ Calories: 992 Cal
- ✓ Fat: 79.21 g
- ✓ Protein: 19.51 g
- ✓ Sugar: 42.49 g

Chocolate Maple Walnuts

This is a super simple recipe that makes a great dinner party dessert that everyone can indulge in as much or as little as they personally choose. The maple syrup plays off the bitterness of the dark chocolate perfectly, and the walnuts provide just the right texture for your guests or family to sink their teeth into.

Preparation Time: 15 minutes
Cooking Time: 30 minutes
Servings: 2 cups od candied walnuts

Ingredients:
- ½ cup pure maple syrup, divided
- 2 cups raw, whole walnuts
- 5 squares of dark chocolate, at least 85%
- 1 ½ tablespoons coconut oil, melted
- 1 tablespoonful of water
- Sifted icing sugar
- 1 teaspoonful of vanilla extract

Directions:
1. Line a large baking sheet with parchment paper.
2. In a medium to large skillet, combine the walnuts and ¼ cup of maple syrup and cook over medium heat, stirring continuously, until walnuts are completely covered with syrup and golden in color, about 3 – 5 minutes.
3. Pour the walnuts onto the parchment paper and separate into individual pieces with a fork. Allow cooling completely, at least 15 minutes.
4. In the meantime, melt the chocolate in a double boiler with the coconut oil. Add the remaining maple syrup and stir until thoroughly combined.
5. When walnuts are cooled, transfer them to a glass bowl and pour the melted chocolate syrup over top. Use a silicone spatula to gently mix until walnuts are completely covered.
6. Transfer back to the parchment paper-lined baking sheet and, once again, separate each of the nuts with a fork.
7. Place the nuts in the fridge for 10 minutes or the freezer for 3 – 5 minutes, until chocolate has completely set.
8. Store in an airtight bag in your fridge.

***Nutrition:** Calories: 2033 Cal | Fat: 124.83 g | Protein: 24.43 g | Sugar: 197.74 g*

Matcha and Chocolate Dipped Strawberries

Chocolate dipped strawberries are possibly one of the most romantic desserts of all time. They're also great for warm summer evenings when you're craving something sweet but don't want a heavy cake or pudding. Eating them any other evening of the year is also just right. You can't go wrong.

Preparation Time: 25 minutes
Cooking Time: 25 minutes
Servings: 4 - 6

Ingredients:
- ✓ 4 tablespoons cocoa butter
- ✓ 4 squares of dark chocolate, at least 85%
- ✓ ¼ cup of coconut oil
- ✓ 1 teaspoon Matcha green tea powder
- ✓ 20 – 25 large whole strawberries, stems on

Directions:
1. Melt cocoa butter, dark chocolate, coconut oil, and Matcha in a double boiler until nearly smooth.
2. Remove from heat and continue stirring until chocolate is completely melted.
3. Pour into a large glass bowl and stir constantly until the chocolate thickens and starts to lose its sheen, about 2 - 5 minutes.
4. Working one at a time, hold the strawberries by stems and dip into chocolate matcha mixture to coat. Let excess drip back into the bowl.
5. Place on a parchment-lined baking sheet and chill dipped berries in the fridge until the shell is set, 20–25 minutes.
6. You may need to reheat matcha mixture if it starts to set before you have dipped all the berries.

Nutrition:
- ✓ Calories: 992 Cal
- ✓ Fat: 101.65 g
- ✓ Protein: 2.9 g
- ✓ Sugar: 17.64 g

Oatmeal Raisin Cookies

Preparation Time: 10 minutes
Cooking Time: 25 minutes
Servings: 4

Ingredients:

- ✓ 1 cup of coconut oil
- ✓ 1 cup of coconut sugar or raw honey
- ✓ 1½ cups almond flour
- ✓ 1 tsp salt
- ✓ ½ tsp grated nutmeg
- ✓ 1 tsp cinnamon
- ✓ 1½ cups raisins
- ✓ 2 large eggs, well beaten
- ✓ 1 tbsp ground vanilla bean
- ✓ 3 cups rolled oats
- ✓ ½ cup chopped walnuts

Directions:

1. Heat oven to 350F.
2. Grease cookie sheets with coconut oil or line with waxed or parchment paper.
3. Mix coconut oil, coconut sugar or raw honey in a large bowl and beat until fluffy.
4. Add vanilla.
5. Beat in eggs.
6. Mix almond flour, salt, cinnamon, and nutmeg in a separate bowl.
7. Stir these dry ingredients into a fluffy mixture.
8. Mix in raisins and nuts.
9. Mix in oats.
10. Spoon out on cookie sheets, leaving 2-inches between cookies.
11. Bake until edges turn golden brown.

Nutrition:

- ✓ Calories: 400 Cal
- ✓ Fat: 27 g
- ✓ Protein: 61.86 g
- ✓ Sugar: 28 g

Coconut Cream Tart

Preparation Time: 10 minutes
Cooking Time: 30 minutes
Servings: 4

Ingredients:

Crust:

- 2 cups almonds, soaked overnight and drained
- 1 cup pitted dates, soaked overnight and drained
- 1 cup chopped dried apricots
- 1½ tsp ground vanilla bean
- 1 banana

Filling:

- 1 cup of flaked coconut
- 1 can of unsweetened coconut milk
- ¾ cup of raw honey
- 3 egg yolks
- 2 tbsp of arrowroot powder
- 2 tbsp of coconut oil
- 2 tsp of ground vanilla bean
- 1/8 tsp of salt
- ½ cup of coconut cream

Directions:

1. Heat the coconut milk, honey, salt and ground vanilla bean over medium heat in a medium-size saucepan.
2. In a separate bowl, whisk the egg yolks and arrowroot powder.
3. Add ½ cup of the warm coconut milk mixture to the egg yolks while whisking constantly. Then pour the egg mixture back into the coconut milk mixture and whisk until the mix thickens and then mix for 3 more minutes.
4. Take off of the heat and mix in the coconut oil and flaked coconut.
5. Cool and pour in the tart crust and refrigerate.
6. Decorate with large coconut flakes.

Nutrition:

- Calories: 325 Cal
- Fat: 23 g
- Protein: 35.76 g
- Sugar: 38 g

Apple Pie

Preparation Time: 10 minutes
Cooking Time: 35 minutes
Servings: 4

Ingredients:

For the crust:
- ✓ 2 Cups of almonds, drenched and drained overnight
- ✓ 1 Cup of pitted dates, soaked and drained overnight
- ✓ 1 Cup of dried apricots peeled
- ✓ 1 1/2 tsp of vanilla ground bean
- ✓ 1 Bananas 1

For Filling the Apple:
- ✓ 2 Tbsp olive oil
- ✓ 9 Apples sour, peeled, cored and cut into 1/4 "thick slices
- ✓ ¼ cup of coconut sugar or raw honey
- ✓ ½ tsp cinnamon
- ✓ 1/8 tsp sea salt
- ✓ ½ cup of coconut milk

For the topping:
- ✓ 1 cup ground nuts and seeds

Directions:
1. *Filling*: melt coconut oil in a large pot over medium heat.
2. Add apples, coconut sugar or raw honey, cinnamon and sea salt.
3. Increase heat to medium-high, and cook, stirring occasionally, until apples release their moisture and melted sugar.
4. Pour coconut milk or cream over apples and continue to cook until apples are soft and liquid has thickened, about 5 minutes, stirring occasionally.
5. Pour the filling into the crust and then top with topping.
6. To avoid burning place a pie shield over the edges of the crust.
7. Bake until topping is just turning golden brown.
8. Cool and serve.

Nutrition:
- ✓ Calories: 212 Cal
- ✓ Fat: 95.12 g
- ✓ Protein: 38.39 g
- ✓ Sugar: 26 g

Blueberry Cream Pie

Preparation Time: 10 minutes
Cooking Time: 30 minutes
Servings: 4

Ingredients:
- Sweet superfoods pie crust filling:
- 2 tsp plant-based gelatin, dissolved in 2 tbsp hot water
- 1/3 cup lemon juice
- 1/3 cup raw honey
- 1 can coconut milk, chilled
- 4 cups blueberries for serving

Directions:
1. Blend the gelatin and the water.
2. Add the lemon juice and stir to dissolve.
3. Whip some 15 minutes of coconut milk and raw honey with the electric mixer.
4. Stir in the whipped cream with the gelatin.
5. Pour the filling into the saucepan.
6. The filling is set in the fridge.
7. Chill until set at 4 hours, and serve with plenty of berries.

Nutrition:
- Calories: 210 Cal
- Fat: 52.62 g
- Protein: 19.61 g
- Sugar: 31 g

Mocha Chocolate Mousse

Everybody appreciates chocolate mousse and this one has a brilliant light and breezy surface. It is brisk and simple to make and is best served the day after it's made.

Preparation Time: 35 minutes
Cooking Time: 2 hours
Servings: 4-6

Ingredients:
- 250g dim chocolate (85% cocoa solids)
- 6 medium unfenced eggs, isolated
- 4 tbsp solid dark espresso
- 4 tbsp almond milk
- Chocolate espresso beans, to enrich

Directions:
1. Soften the chocolate in a huge bowl set over a skillet of delicately stewing water, ensuring the base of the bowl doesn't contact the water. Expel the bowl from the heat and leave the dissolved chocolate to cool to room temperature.
2. When the softened chocolate is at room temperature, race in the egg yolks each in turn and afterwards tenderly overlap in the espresso and almond milk.
3. Utilizing a hand-held electric blender, whisk the egg whites until firm pinnacles structure, at that point blend several tablespoons into the chocolate blend to release it. Delicately overlap in the rest of, an enormous metal spoon.
4. Move the mousse to singular glasses and smooth the surface. Spread with stick film and chill for in any event 2 hours, preferably medium-term. Enliven with chocolate espresso beans before serving.

Nutrition:
- Calories: 112 Cal
- Fat: 29.89 g
- Protein: 40.3 g
- Sugar: 128.13 g

Mediterranean Scones

Preparation Time: 10 minutes
Cooking Time: 10 minutes
Servings: 4

Ingredients:
For the scones:
- ✓ 250 g of flour
- ✓ 1 teaspoon of baking soda
- ✓ 2 teaspoons of cream of tartar
- ✓ 40 g of butter
- ✓ 150 ml of milk
- ✓ 1 egg
- ✓ salt
- ✓ black pepper

For the stuffing:
- ✓ 2 mozzarella cheese
- ✓ 1 red pepper
- ✓ 4 spoons of olives
- ✓ 3 spoons of desalted capers
- ✓ basil
- ✓ flax seed
- ✓ oil
- ✓ salt

Directions:
1. We prepare the scones by mixing the baking soda and cream of tartar with the flour. We combine a pinch of salt, plenty of black pepper, the cold butter into chunks and knead quickly to obtain a sandy mixture. We add the lightly beaten egg and mix, then we also add the milk, all at once. We mix the mixture and put it on a floured surface. We form 10 little balls bigger than a walnut and we crush them arranging them on a baking sheet. Bake at 220 ° C for about 10 minutes.
2. We cut the peppers into strips and sauté them in the pan with the oil and basil, add salt. We toast the flax seeds in a pan. We divide the scones in half and we will make them with mozzarella, peppers, olives and capers. Add a drizzle of oil and a sprinkling of flax seeds and cook again in the oven for a few minutes before serving.

Nutrition: *Calories: 137 Cal | Fat: 48.32 g | Protein: 36.35 g | Sugar: 4.16 g*

Chapter 20: Exercises to Do

The Sirtfood Diet is designed to help you activate your sirtuin genes without the necessity of exercise or fasting, but that doesn't mean you shouldn't add regular and consistent physical activity to your life to protect your body from deterioration and aging in other ways.

Your nutrition can do the lion's share of maintaining health and preventing disease but if you don't use your body and muscles on a regular basis, they will atrophy, stiffen up and stop working for you.

What this means primarily is that exercise doesn't have to be your go-to solution for weight loss or weight management, but rather it should be practiced as a means of maintaining our ability to move and stay strong and energetic. Our bodies were designed to go through a wide range of movements, from the bending, pulling and lifting required to farm, gather and harvest, to the cardiovascular capacity to hunt and the combination of all of the above that is required to keep children occupied and safe.

In short, even if a Sirtfood Diet helps you fight disease and reach your ideal body weight, you shouldn't neglect your exercise.

Moderate Movement

Walking is one type of physical activity that is considered moderate and most people are able to do it, though distance and speed may vary.

You've probably heard of the social movement in which people around the world are encouraged to track their steps and work towards a goal of 10,000 steps a day.

One study looked at a healthy, youthful population of students and asked one group to meet these 10,000 steps per day goal and another group to simplify their lives with elevators, wheelchairs, and plenty of sitting, reducing their steps per day to a mere 2,000 steps. Within 2 weeks, the less active group lost an average of 5% of their muscle mass (TEDx, 2014).

As a society, many of us are not even reaching 2,000 steps per day.
You're reading this because you want to change your life through your diet, and sirtfoods are beautifully designed to help you do just that. It would be a mistake, however, to think that you don't still have to spend some of your time each day moving your body.

The reality is that humans were designed to eat nutritiously in order to move effectively. If we eliminate either or both of those factors from the equation of our lives, we are going to feel the effects in the form of disease, weight gain and the breakdown of our bodies. Being able to move is a joy that we should not take for granted.

With the Sirtfood Diet in your corner, there should be no need to exercise as a means of keeping your weight at an optimal level, however, it can help you find that level more quickly.

From the start, this has been more about creating and maintaining health for you, rather than simply focusing on weight. If we look at all the chronic diseases that we're trying to prevent, such as heart disease, diabetes, and cancer, we should be doing anything we can think of to prevent these tragic conditions from claiming our lives.

There's almost unlimited scientific evidence that physical activity can reduce your risk for all of these diseases. We know that a large part of that protection is because our sirtuin genes are activated. Just because sirtfoods can also activate those genes doesn't mean we should assume physical activity is no longer necessary.

Instead, we should consider the compounded benefits of integrating both a sirtfood rich diet with moderate physical activity on a regular basis.

We should be enjoying the gift of movement more than anything, whenever we have the opportunity. It doesn't need to be an exhausting activity and you shouldn't hate doing it. It is supposed to make you feel energized, relaxed and content. Government guidelines suggest a mere 2.5 hours of moderate activity per week that works out to less than 30 minutes per day. Moderate activity can be almost anything you enjoy doing, walking your dog or joining an adult amateur sports team.

You will want to monitor your physical activity to some extent during the first phase of the Sirtfood Diet, because you will consume less calories than your body is used to No need to put your body under more stress. But as described here moderate movement can absolutely enhance your first-stage experience and results.

Once you're consuming a regular number of calories again, but enjoying the significantly improved health benefits of a diet loaded with sirtfoods, you're even encouraged to increase your current physical activity to add more long-term health to your life.

Muscle and Strength

When you're completely sedentary, doing nothing but lounging in front of your television or working at a computer desk, your muscles require about 30% of the energy your body needs to keep you just sitting there.

When you exercise, your muscles use closer to 90% of your energy. As you can imagine, this will burn up a lot more carbohydrates and fat than simply sitting in your chair, but you knew that already.

The less you use your muscles, the smaller and weaker they will get but again, this is not news.

Why is muscle mass and strength so important to our health?

One reason is that studies show that the risk of death for individuals classified as "strong" is about half that of those classified as "weak" amongst all causes of mortality. The stronger you are, the more likely you are to remain alive. That is definitely motivating.

65 It's not old and we should all expect to live that long at least, and many of us are much longer.

But 65 years of inactivity is a long time to let your muscles shrink, and this is a major contributing factor to chronic disease prevalence at this age.

One particular shocking disease is sarcopenia, which is the age-related waste of our muscles. As we age, after reaching our 30s, we naturally start losing muscle mass and strength at a rate of about 3 percent or more per decade. This is, besides the muscle, that we simply lose from being sedentary. Usually, that muscles traded in for fat.

Muscle mass is not purely designed for aesthetic purposes. It is associated with both our balance and our bone density, which can lead to frailty and loss of independence in our future.

But it isn't just in our retirement years that a lack of muscle will start to really affect us. Diseases such as cancer, renal failure, heart disease, and rheumatoid and osteoarthritis are all linked to lower muscle mass, both as a cause and as a result.

We know sirtfoods can help protect our muscle mass, but how should we build it?
The moderate movement suggestions are ideal during the first phase of the Sirtfood Diet, or any time in your life you're reducing calories for any other reason. But we will need to dedicate more energy specifically to our muscles to live a full, healthy, and strong life.

Our bodies are designed to adapt to what transforms into a normal motion. If you've never gone into your life before for a jog, the first block will be a fight. But if you practice every day, your body will adapt and it will become easy to jog 1 block.

If you have never lifted a baby before and you find yourself having to carry one around for 8 -10 hours a day, even a tiny 7-pound newborn is going to feel heavy at first. But after a few weeks of parenthood, your body will adapt, you will become stronger, and even when your baby weighs 20 pounds, you won't find them too heavy to manage.

We are not all going to be carrying around growing babies all our lives, however, so a smart way to grow your muscles using the same principle is to either lift weights or use your bodyweight.

Using weights gives you the ability to track any improvements in strength as you find yourself progressively adding more weight to your lifting. However, bodyweight exercises have the distinct advantage of not requiring any equipment and they use dynamic movements, which also help to improve total body wellness, flexibility, and mobility.

Bodyweight exercises include movements like pushups, pullups, squats, and lunges, taking the stairs and even holding much yoga poses.

You don't have to give your entire life over to becoming an athlete. You can see dramatic results in as little as 3 days a week, only 30 minutes at a time.

If you begin progressively building strength from a younger age, you will protect yourself against many so-called chronic and age-related diseases. If you are already in the range of 65+ years of age, all is not lost.

If you start challenging your muscles now, with your doctor's permission and guidance, you can build them up again and start recovering from any muscle loss-related illnesses you may already have. You will need to start slowly and carefully, but in just a few weeks of training, the results can quickly change your outlook on life.

A Sirtfood diet will help to protect the muscle you have, but to really combat this natural process, you should be dedicated to actively strengthening your muscles throughout your entire life. Lifting weights or doing progressively more challenging bodyweight exercises is a great way to build your muscles.

Chapter 21: Phase One Meal Plan

Phase 1: 7 pounds in 7 days

The phase 1 of the Sirtfood diet is the one that will allow you to take the first successful step towards achieving a leaner shape and a healthier glow.

The authors of the diet proved with their clinical trial, that no matter your initial weight or gender, you will lose 7 pounds in 7 days, and it won't be muscle mass!
This is actually not the most amazing part of the diet, the fact that the lost pounds won't come back to haunt you is! After all, the first week of the diet is based on the simple, well-proven base of calorie restriction, but with the added twist of a sirtfood-laden meal plan.

Not only will you see an improvement of your shape, but you will feel more vital, your skin will achieve a natural glow that no cream can ever compete with. I was skeptical at first too, but I never felt so energetic, clean, and beautiful.

Phase 1 of the diet is the one that produces the greatest results. Over the course of seven days, you will follow a simple method in order to lose 3.5 kg.
During the first three days, the intake of calories will have to be limited to one thousand per day at most. Basically, you can have three green juices and a solid meal, all based on Sirt foods. From day 4 to 7, the daily calories will become fifteen hundred. Every day you will eat two green juices and two solid Sirt-meals.

By the end of the seven days, you should have lost, on average, 3.5 kilos.
Despite the reduction in calories, the participants do not feel hungry, and the calorie limit is an indication rather than a goal. Even in the most intensive phase, calorie restriction is not as drastic as in many other regimes. Sirtfoods have a naturally satiating effect so that many of you will feel pleasantly full and satisfied.

Phase 1 plan:

Days 1 to 3 – max. 1000 calories

- ✓ 3 green juices
- ✓ 1 main Sirtfood meal

Think of this first 3 days as the reset button for your metabolism. I swear it isn't as grueling as it seems. The match in the green juice and the SIRT-activating of the foods will satisfy and make you feel more energetic than ever.

Days 4 to 7 – max. 1500 calories

- ✓ 2 Green juices
- ✓ 2 main Sirtfood meals

Tips to get started

1. Get a good juicer

One necessary kitchen tool that you will need aside from the actual foods is a juicer. You will need a juicer as soon as you start the Sirtfood diet. Juicers are everywhere so they are quite easy to find, but the quality ranges greatly, however.
This is where price, function, and convenience come into play. You could go to a popular department store, or you can find them online. Once you know what you are going after, you can shop around.

The quality of the juicer will also determine the nutritional quality and sometimes the taste of your juice, which we will explain in a bit. Just know that buying a cheap juicer may seem like a good idea now, but if you decide to upgrade then you will have spent more money, and twice. If you buy a good juicer, think of it as an investment into your health. Many people have spent money on a gym membership that went unused for quadruple the cost of one juicer. A juicer won't go to waste.

Note: If all else fails, in a pinch and with a blender you could get away with an (albeit very poor quality) juice by blending the foods, and using a fine mesh to filter the juice that is left. The only problem is that you would be getting a fraction of the nutrients, and also probably a spike in sugar, as very little fiber will be in the juice to help slow down the natural sugar absorption. Use caution.

2. Stock your fridge and pantry

First, clear your cabinets and refrigerator of foods that are obviously unhealthy and that might tempt you. You also will have a very low-calorie intake at the start, and you do not want to be tempted into a quick fix that may set you back. Even though you will have new recipes, you may feel that your old comfort foods are easier at the moment.

Then, go shopping for all of the ingredients that you will need for the week. If you buy what you will need it is more cost-effective. Also, once you see the recipes, you will notice that there are many ingredients that overlap. You will get to know your portions as you proceed with the diet but at least you will have what you need and save yourself some trips to the store.

Wash, dry, cut and store all of the foods that you need, that way you have them conveniently prepared when you need them. This will make a new diet seem less tedious.

3.   Prepare in advance

A resolution for a change in diet is often thwarted by the lack of time. So, knowing this, prepare. You can easily prepare the meals the night before to take to work the day after instead of getting tempted by a cafeteria sandwich. Juices can be prepared in bulk and stored. They will keep in the fridge for 3 days and even longer in the freezer. It is very important that you protect them from light and add the matcha only when you are ready to consume them.

4.   Get used to eating early

Drink your juices as the earlier meals in the day if it helps you. For three reasons: It's a great way to start your day. (1) It will give you energy for breakfast and for lunch especially. By not having to digest heavy foods, your body saves time and energy usually spent on moving things around to go through all the laborious motions. You will be guaranteed to feel lighter and more energetic this way. You can always change this pattern after the maintenance phase, but you may find that you want to keep that schedule. (2) Having fruits and vegetables before starchy or cooked meals, no matter how healthy the ingredients, is the best way to go for your digestion. Fruits and vegetables digest more rapidly, and the breakdown into the compounds that we can use more readily. Think of it as having your salad before your dinner. It works in the same way. The heavier foods, grains, oils, meats, etc., take more time to digest. If you eat these first, they will slow things down and that is where you have a backup of food needing to be broken down. This is also when you may find yourself with indigestion. (3)

Juices, especially green juices contain phytochemicals that not only serve as anti-oxidants but they contribute to our energy and mood. You will notice that you feel much differently after drinking a green juice than you would if you had eggs and sausage. You may want to make a food diary and note things such as this!

Even without following the Sirtfood diet, eating early in the day is the healthier choice. Our busy lives often don't allow for a proper breakfast, but Sirtfoods give some great option for a quick breakfast on-the-go (smoothies, pre-prepared muesli, easy scrambled eggs and tofu). Sirtfoods supercharge our energies, so you have all the more to gain by getting them early in the morning. The day won't feel quite as long as it used to!

5.   Be mindful of what you are drinking

Besides the mandatory green juices, you should feel free to drink freely: plain water, black coffee, and green tea are recommended. Do not drink soft drinks and fruit juices! To make your water tastier and more "SIRT-full" you can add some sliced strawberries to cold sparkling water.

Don't change your coffee habits: caffeine withdrawal can be grueling and, likewise, you shouldn't start drinking it if you are not a habitual consumer. Do try to drink your coffee black. Clinical researchers have discovered that milk can impair the absorption of the SIRT-activating nutrients, the same goes for green tea. Add a slice of lemon to your green tea instead it will increase the absorption of the nutrients that stimulate SIRT.

For this first week include red wine only as a cooking ingredient.

6. Eat until you are 80% full

It's an Okinawan proverb and it couldn't be truer. Sirtfoods will more than satisfy your appetite, you might even find yourself feeling full before finishing your meal, don't force it down!

7. Think of the journey and not the destination

This is not a diet to lose weight, it's a change in lifestyle and a celebration of the most diverse culinary traditions. Take joy in cooking and knowing that you are eating well. Focus on the path, rather than the destination and you will find it much easier to follow the diet.

Phase Two Meal Plan

This part of the first week is less radical than the other one, but it involves lowering your green juice intake from three servings to just two. You can have one green juice at 9:00 a.m., and the second one at 4:00 p.m. (for instance), but you can adjust the schedule according to your time.
But don't worry. As you will compensate with an extra main meal, you will have two meals per day during this phase. You should be able to keep the same dessert (the dark chocolate with 85 percent cocoa), and you will have again the option to choose from a standard or vegan meal.

Day 4

For this day, you will have included in your menu two standard meals and two vegan meals. You can choose to have both meals standard or both meals vegan, but if you want to mix them (to have one meal vegan and the other one standard), feel free to do so. You can have your breakfast at 7:00 a.m. and the second meal at 1:00 p.m.

Therefore, these are the standard meals: sirt muesli, which is a proper breakfast meal, and salmon fillet with caramelized endive, celery leaf, and arugula salad. (Don't forget to pour some extra-virgin olive oil on the salad.)

As for the vegan meals, you can have sirt muesli (vegan style) and Tuscan bean stew.

Day 5

For this day, you can stick to the same juice drinking and eating schedule. The only difference is that you are trying different meals than the day before.
For the standard diet, you can have strawberry buckwheat tabbouleh and stir-fried greens with miso-marinated baked cod. For the vegan menu, you can try vegan strawberry buckwheat tabbouleh and buckwheat noodles in miso broth with celery, kale, and tofu.

Day 6

There isn't too much difference between day 6 and the prior days of phase 2. Just stick to the same green juices and the same schedule for having them, or you can have the meals.

When it comes to the standard food preference, you can have sirt super salad and grilled beef with herb-roasted potatoes, onion rings, garlic kale, and red wine. (Now this sounds too delicious, so you have to try it.)

But if you are not into beef, then perhaps you want to go with the vegan menu: lentil sirt super salad and baked potato with kidney bean mole.

Day 7

You are finishing the seven-day meal plan in style, as this day has included extremely delicious meals. You already have the scheduled set for your meals and green juices, plus you still have a small piece of dark chocolate (after each meal) to sweeten your day (not that it requires sweetening).

If you want to choose the standard meals, you can go with the sirtfood omelet, baked chicken breast with walnut, and red onion and parsley pesto salad (some extra-virgin olive oil is recommended). If you feel like you want to try the vegan menu, you can have vegan Waldorf salad and roasted eggplant wedges with walnut and tomato and parsley pesto salad (don't forget to add extra-virgin olive oil).

The menu suggested during these days can be used as guidelines, but it is up to you if you want to stick to having these meals exactly on the same days as mentioned in the plan. Perhaps you want to try the meal from day 1 on day 3, and the other way around. I wouldn't recommend trying a meal from day 5 or day 6 in phase 1 of the seven-day meal plan. Therefore, feel free to play with the meals, but make sure you don't have a meal that is for phase 2 of the first week in phase 1 or the other way around. You will need to pay attention to quantity as well.

These foods may sound delicious, but you can't have a huge portion. You really need to stick with the quantity mentioned in the recipes. Speaking of recipes, I mentioned some standard and vegan meals, but I haven't said anything about how to prepare them. Well, don't worry! This collection will have plenty of recipes you can use during this meal plan.

Conclusion

When you first switch to a clean diet it can be difficult to understand which foods are clean foods and which ones are not. When buying fresh foods always aim for the organic varieties, but if this is not possible then any fresh food is better than the processed option.

To help you plan your food shopping, the following lists show a variety of clean foods which you can incorporate into your meal plans.

Fresh Fruit & Vegetables
- All varieties of fresh fruit and vegetables, including raw, frozen fruit and vegetables should be incorporated into your clean diet to ensure a good variety of natural vitamins and minerals. If possible, buy organic produce as it is free from pesticides.
- Although most fruits contain sugar, this is a natural sugar and far healthier than the refined sugars found in processed foods.

Meat & Fish
All types of meat and fish are suitable for a clean diet but there are a few guidelines you should be aware of.
- **Beef:** This is best to buy directly from a butcher as you should choose only grass-fed and humanely raised beef.
- **Pork:** The majority of pork products are processed so avoid ham and cheaper cuts of pork, gammon and bacon. Stick to only the high-quality pork options. Again, a butcher's is the best place to purchase pork as you can gain information as to its quality.
- **Fish:** Always buy fish that has been caught sustainably and limit high mercury content fish to 2 servings per week.

High mercury content fish includes:
- *King Mackerel*
- *Marlin*
- *Shark*
- *Swordfish*
- *Tuna*

Poultry & Eggs
All eggs and poultry are a good source of protein but choose the free-range, organic options whenever possible.

Many of the cheaper super store varieties of fresh chicken will have added water which cannot be considered as clean food.
Check for products that state no added water or even salt!

Dairy Products
- **Milk:** Always choose full-fat varieties and stick to organic milk whenever possible. For a clean alternative, you could switch to pure, unsweetened, organic coconut milk, canned varieties not cartons, or unsweetened organic soy milk.

- **Cheese:** Block cheeses only and full-fat varieties. Never buy pre-shredded cheeses or low-fat version and stick to the better-quality cheeses.

- **Cottage Cheese**: Only good quality, full-fat varieties.

- **Yoghurt:** Full-fat plain yoghurts. If you prefer flavored yoghurt mix a little whole or pureed fruit into the plain yoghurt.

Beans, Pulses & Seeds
All beans, lentils, chickpeas etc. can be included in recipes
For a little variety to your recipes try adding sunflower, flax or sesame seeds.

Unrefined Grains
- **Wheat:** Use whole meal varieties of bread, pasta and rice. If possible, stick to organic.

- **Oats:** Use unflavored rolled oats or steel-cut oats in recipes.

- **Flour:** Always use whole wheat flours when cooking and for an alternative to wheat you can use unprocessed coconut or almond flour.

Cooking Oils
Choose natural oils such as Olive Oil, Coconut oil, and Avocado Oil.

Herbs & Spices
Always choose fresh or dried herbs and spices and avoid seasoning packets. I would recommend spending a little time and money stocking a great herbs and spice store at home. They will come in so handy when preparing clean meals.

Natural Sweeteners
- **Honey:** Organic when possible
- **Pure syrup:** Avoid processed bottles and buy organic where possible.

Condiments

- Always choose no added sugar varieties

- **Ketchup & Mustard:** It is possible to purchase clean varieties but these are often very difficult to find. The cleanest option is to make your own.

Thank you for reading!

I hope that you find the success you are looking for.

I hope this guide has helped you become acquainted with the Sirtfood diet and achieve your weight loss and health goals.

Good luck on your sirtfood journey!

CPSIA information can be obtained
at www.ICGtesting.com
Printed in the USA
LVHW061556110621
689237LV00013BA/1052